How to Apply Dynamics Processing

How to Apply
Dynamics Processing

Craig Anderton

ROWMAN & LITTLEFIELD
Lanham • Boulder • New York • London

Published by Rowman & Littlefield
An imprint of The Rowman & Littlefield Publishing Group, Inc.
4501 Forbes Boulevard, Suite 200, Lanham, Maryland 20706
www.rowman.com

6 Tinworth Street, London SE11 5AL, United Kingdom

Copyright © 2019 by Craig Anderton

All rights reserved. No part of this book may be reproduced in any form or by any electronic or mechanical means, including information storage and retrieval systems, without written permission from the publisher, except by a reviewer who may quote passages in a review.

Library of Congress Cataloging-in-Publication Data is available upon request.

♾️™ The paper used in this publication meets the minimum requirements of American National Standard for Information Sciences—Permanence of Paper for Printed Library Materials, ANSI/NISO Z39.48-1992.

Printed in the United States of America

Contents

Acknowledgments ix

Introduction. About This Book 1
    The Importance of Dynamics Processing 1
    Tips and References 2

Chapter 1. Dynamics Basics 3
    The Beginning of Dynamics Control 4
    The Decibel 5
        Headroom in Digital Systems 5
        The Decibel and Dynamic Range Control 6
    Manual Gain-Riding 6
    Level-Riding Plug-Ins 7
    Common Dynamics Processor Parameters 8
        Input Level 8
        Threshold 8
        Ratio 9
        Knee 9
        Ceiling 9
        Output Level (also called Gain or Makeup Gain) 9
        Automatic Output Level 9
        Mix 9
        Attack 9
        Release (also called Decay) 10
        Auto Attack and Release 10
        Adaptive Attack and Release 10
        Hold 10
        Metering 10
        Lookahead 12
        Stereo Link 12
        Algorithm 12
        Sidechain Controls 12
        Mid-Side Processing 13
    Key Takeaways 13

Chapter 2. Dynamics Processing Devices 15

Limiter 15
    Limiter Parameters and Controls 16
    How to Adjust the Parameters 19
    Parameter Adjustment Tips 20

Compressor 20
    Compressor Parameters 21
    How to Adjust the Parameters 25
    Parameter Adjustment Tips 26
    Compressor Presets: Friend or Foe? 27

Multiband Compressor 32
    Multiband Compressor Controls 33
    How to Adjust the Parameters 33
    Parameter Adjustment Tips 34

Loudness Maximizer 35
    How to Adjust the Parameters 36

Expander 37
    Expander Parameters 37
    How to Adjust the Parameters 38

Transient Shaper 39
    How to Adjust the Parameters 41

Noise Gate 41
    Noise Gate Parameters 42
    How to Adjust the Parameters 43

Dynamic Equalization 44
Key Takeaways 45

Chapter 3. Sidechaining and De-Essing 47

How to Access the Sidechain Input 48
Ways to Sidechain 49
    Duplicate a Track 49
    Insert a Send 49
Internal vs. External Sidechaining 50
De-Essing 50
    De-Esser Parameters 51
Key Takeaways 52

Contents   **vii**

Chapter 4. Dynamics Control with DSP 53
    Normalization 53
        Normalizing Individual Tracks on Albums 54
        Normalizing Comped Instrument or Vocal Parts 54
        "Manual Limiting" with Normalization 55
        Phrase-by-Phrase Normalization 56
    Dynamics via Automation 59
        What You Can Automate 59
        Automating Signal Processor Parameters 59
        Automation Basics 59
        Automation Methods 61
        Clip Gain Automation 63
    Key Takeaways 64

Chapter 5. Dynamics Processor Applications 65
    Processing on the Master Bus 65
    Why You May Not Want to Compress the Master Bus When Mixing 66
    Multiband Dynamics for Bass 66
    Reduce Amp Sim Harshness with De-Essing 68
    Dynamics Processing and Signal Chain Position 69
        Dynamics Processing and EQ 70
        Compression Before or After Distortion 70
        Noise Gate Before or After Distortion 70
        Limiter Before or After Compressor 71
        Limiter Before Amp Sim 71
        Dynamics Control Before or After Envelope-Controlled Filter 71
    A Better Guitar Sustainer 71
        Noise Gate Attack Delay 72
    Interfacing Electric Instruments with Studio Dynamics Processors 73
    Transparent Compression 74
    A One-Knob Compressor 75
    Sidechain Applications 77
        Locking Kick Drum and Bass Together 77
        Pumped Drums 77
        Frequency-Selective Compression 79
        Frequency-Selective Drum Pumping 80
        Ducking a Music Bed with Narration 82
        Gentler Sidechain Gating 83

The Compressor/Limiting "Delta" Test 84
Drum Enhancement 85
Key Takeaways..86

Appendix. The "Loudness Wars" and Measuring Dynamics 87
Measuring Dynamics..88
More Metering 89
Yes, Dynamics are Back..90

Acknowledgments

A series like this is never the work of one person, but rather a collection of the experiences obtained over the years from too many people to acknowledge here. Yet some deserve a special mention.

Dan Earley, my editor at Music Sales, who was the first person to say, "You know what would be cool? A series of books on recording, like those Time Life libraries." Well Dan, better late than never, right?

Sir George Martin, who was kind enough to write the foreword to my 1977 book, *Home Recording for Musicians*. He asked for samples of my writing, and I thought that would be the end of it. Instead, he wrote an eloquent foreword that set a wonderful tone for the book. He truly was the consummate gentleman everyone says he was.

The team at Hal Leonard—especially John Cerullo, who green-lighted this series and brought in Frank D. Cook to serve as the editor for these books.

My father, who taught me that it didn't matter if I was a dreadful writer as long as I could edit my words into something readable—and who also showed me what it meant to love music.

My mother, who with my father was unfailingly supportive when I wanted to do things like drop out of college, join a rock band, go on tour, and never look back!

My brother, who understood music on a very deep level and died too young.

And of course, the many *(many)* engineers and producers who let me look over their shoulders and absorb knowledge like a sponge over the past five decades. My hope is that this series will help pass their collective wisdom on to another generation.

Introduction

About This Book

Welcome to the book series Musician's Guide to Home Recording. This series of short publications was written to address the needs of musicians and recording enthusiasts who are interested in creating self-produced songs or doing audio production work for others.

Rather than trying to cover all aspects of recording in a single sprawling volume, each title in the series concisely and accessibly addresses a particular subject. You can select individual titles to hone in on certain skills or proceed through the entire series; this kind of approach lets you develop a comprehensive knowledge at your own pace.

This book, *How to Apply Dynamics Processing*, covers one of the most important families of signal processors, whether virtual or hardware-based, in today's studio.

The Importance of Dynamics Processing

Dynamics processing began as a way to shoehorn the wide dynamic range of live audio into the restricted dynamic range of radio transmitters, tape recorders, and vinyl. But in today's world of digital audio, dynamics processing can be an important creative tool—not just a way to solve problems.

In the past few decades, dynamics processing has grown by leaps and bounds. There are software emulations of classic hardware dynamics processors, entirely new types of dynamics processors that have no precedent, processors designed specifically for mastering or mixing, and more. You'll also find dynamics processors in keyboards, guitar multieffects, and other pieces of gear.

With all these options, it's increasingly important to choose the processor that will provide the ideal solution for your recording, mixing, and mastering needs. This book describes the basics of dynamics processing, the different available processing types and technologies, the purpose of sidechaining, ways to control dynamics with the DSP inside today's virtual studio software, and other applications. Armed with this knowledge, you'll feel confident about using dynamics processing to enhance your music in the best possible way.

The more you know about the technology behind the scenes, the more easily you can take advantage of it to do your bidding—and to make better music.

Tips and References

This book includes various tips, definitions, cross-references, and other supplemental nuggets throughout its pages. These are denoted with the following icons and formatting.

 Tips and side notes provide helpful hints and suggestions, background information, or additional details on a concept or topic.

 Definitions provide explanations of technical terms, industry jargon, or abbreviations.

 Cross-References alert you to another section, book, or online resource that provides additional information on the current topic.

 Warnings caution you against conditions that may have adverse effects or unexpected results.

Chapter 1

Dynamics Basics

Dynamic range is the difference between a sound's loudest and softest levels. Our ears have an incredibly wide dynamic range; we can hear extremely soft and loud sounds (although excessively loud sounds can damage our hearing). Detecting quiet sounds was sometimes a matter of survival (is that grass rustling in the wind, or a sabertooth tiger looking for lunch?), while loud sounds signified something big and important (possibly even earth-shaking).

Dynamics are also an essential part of music and help convey emotion. Quiet sections draw us in, and loud sections surprise us. Music is often a balance between change and consistency, and it's also a balance between loud and soft.

With today's music technology, just as equalizers can control tonal balance, dynamics processors can control dynamic range. Dynamics processors became essential for broadcasting to prevent a problem called overmodulation, but also were well suited to studio recording because live music's extremely wide dynamic range was impossible to capture on tape or vinyl. Dynamics control could restrict dynamic range by keeping levels soft enough to prevent overloading the tape or causing a phonograph needle to jump out of its groove, but loud enough to rise above tape hiss or vinyl's surface noise.

Now we're in the digital age, and 24-bit digital audio recording offers dynamic range that goes well beyond vinyl, tape, and even the CD's 16-bit dynamic range (which nonetheless is more than enough for excellent audio fidelity). Thanks to high-quality input and output electronics, we can record very high and low levels.

Yet dynamics processing continues to play an important role in the studio for many reasons, like being able to prevent distortion that could otherwise ruin a recording, provide more overall "punch" to a production (if not overused), or serve as a creative effect that has little to do with traditional dynamics control. Dynamics processing can also help players who lack a good *touch* (the ability to play an instrument with controlled nuances). For example, a singer with good mic technique will move closer or farther away from the mic to keep relatively constant levels. An inexperienced singer with less developed technique might unintentionally create level variations that, unlike level changes designed to enhance the music, could cause vocal passages to be uneven. Dynamics processing can help compensate for this issue.

Bassists often use compression because the ear is less sensitive in the bass range, so subtle dynamics may not be heard clearly. Giving the bass a more even dynamic range can provide a fuller low end, which makes it easier to hear the bass part. Restricting dynamic range to make soft parts louder can also bring music above the background noise of everyday life (like road noise when listening in cars).

Commercials use a particularly annoying variant on dynamics control to increase the perceived loudness as much as technically possible. Soundtracks alter dynamics to keep music from competing too much with dialog. And broadcasts control dynamics to prevent distortion.

How much dynamics processing to use can be a controversial subject. Many listeners think "louder is better," so pop music recordings often have a super-compressed dynamic range (sometimes to the point of destroying dynamics altogether). For DJs, compressed dance music minimizes level variations, thus giving more control over level via the DJ mixer's faders. Classical and jazz recordings use little or no dynamics processing. (Fortunately, at least for broadcasting and streaming audio, creating music at the loudest possible level is becoming less important, for reasons described in the Appendix.)

For all of these applications, it's important to choose the right type of dynamics processing—and we have plenty of options. Let's start by looking at a brief history of dynamics processing.

The Beginning of Dynamics Control

During the early days of radio broadcasting, a signal that was too loud would overmodulate a transmitter. This could not only lead to distortion, but would sometimes cause the transmitter to go off-air briefly (or in extreme cases, would lead to equipment failure). The only way to prevent this was for the radio studio's engineer to try and anticipate level changes, and then alter the signal's level manually. This process, called *gain-riding*, was an imprecise solution. No matter how skilled the engineer, it was never possible to ride gain perfectly.

Devices called *peak limiters* became commercially available from RCA and Western Electric in the 1930s. They limited peaks so that excessively loud signals wouldn't hit the transmitter. Like invisible hands that could sense peaks, they turned down the gain automatically. In the '40s, a device invented years earlier by Al Towne called the PROGAR (Program Guardian) hit the market. It combined a *compressor* with automatic gain control and limiting. The compressor didn't just limit peaks; it also smoothed out volume levels to make them more consistent. The limiter handled any remaining peaks.

Although electronic limiting was a major advance over human gain-riding, the limiter couldn't turn down a level until it sensed a level change, and by that time the beginning of a peak had already occurred. The next improvement happened when General Electric combined a peak limiter with a delay line so that the peak limiter could anticipate level changes. It could then turn down the peaks when they happened, instead of slightly afterward.

Compression and limiting were also ideal for the burgeoning recording industry to accommodate the restricted bandwidth of vinyl and tape. Shortly thereafter, dynamics processing morphed into a tool for creative special effects, as well as into more refined versions of traditional dynamics control devices.

Today, it's important to know how to use dynamics in both traditional and non-traditional ways. Regardless, dynamics processors are still variations on an "invisible hand" that can work faster and more accurately than humans.

Before getting into the various types of dynamics processors, let's look at some audio terms that help us understand how dynamic range processors work.

The Decibel

There are several different kinds of decibel (dB), and a complete treatment of this specification could take up a book—so let's deal with the dB in general terms. Reduced to essentials, the dB is a unit of *ratio* between the level of two audio signals.

Headroom in Digital Systems

Because the decibel represents a ratio, we need a standard signal to which we can compare other signals—in other words, if a signal is half as loud as another signal, that's useful information, but it doesn't tell us about the signal levels in absolute terms. In many cases involving dynamics control, the reference is to the maximum level a system can handle, which is called 0 dB or the *ceiling*. For example, you'll see signal levels referenced as –3 dB, –6 dB, –20 dB, etc. The negative numbers show how far these values are below 0 dB.

The audio engine inside your recording program has an almost unlimited dynamic range. However, audio going into or coming out of your computer passes through hardware—and even modern audio hardware doesn't have an infinite dynamic range. To prevent distortion caused by exceeding the hardware's dynamic range, it's good practice to allow for some *headroom*—the difference in level between a signal's peak and the maximum level a preamp, analog-to-digital converter, or digital-to-analog converter can handle. Levels that exceed the maximum amount of headroom will result in distortion. (Digital distortion is particularly nasty because it sounds harsher than the distortion associated with tube amps and some analog circuitry.)

Most audio interfaces have some kind of metering to indicate the incoming signal's strength (Fig. 1.1).

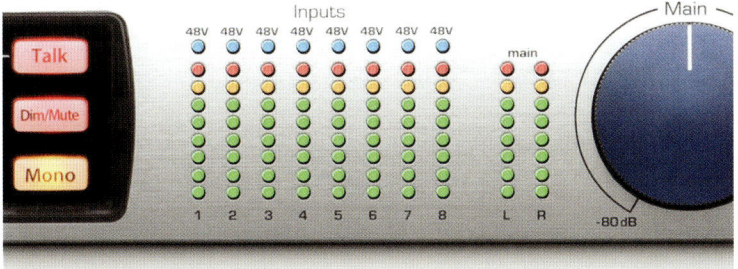

Figure 1.1 The Studio 192 interface from PreSonus includes multi-step LED meters for each channel to monitor the input level. Green LEDs indicate acceptable levels, yellow LEDs mean close to clipping, and red LEDs warn that clipping is occurring.

At the very least, the interface will include a clipping indicator—typically an LED that glows red if the signal exceeds the available headroom. This is your cue to turn down the level coming into the interface.

More sophisticated metering can indicate the signal level with more precision. For example, if the peaks light an LED labeled –6 dB, then there's 6 dB of headroom prior to the onset of distortion.

 When recording, many engineers recommend setting digital audio levels at least 6 dB below 0 (peak levels of –12 dB or –15 dB are common) for two reasons. First, this will accommodate unanticipated peaks. Second, some engineers believe the performance of audio gear can degrade at the limits of its operation.

On playback, leaving some headroom avoids the possibility of *intersample distortion,* as explained later in this chapter.

The Decibel and Dynamic Range Control

Already we have a useful application for dynamics control: making sure the signal peaks don't exceed 0 dB when entering a recording system (the same is true of playback—the output signal can't exceed the playback medium's maximum dynamic range). This requires an electronic circuit that constantly monitors the input level. If the level exceeds 0 dB, the circuit quickly and automatically turns down the gain so the signal won't exceed 0 dB. In a nutshell, that's what some of the most common dynamics processors do. But before we get into today's modern dynamics processors, let's look at more traditional options.

Manual Gain-Riding

In a way, the ultimate "manual gain-riding" is the dynamics inherent in a musician's playing. Although we now have sophisticated electronic devices to control dynamics, there are still two situations where manual gain-riding is common.

Sometimes after setting levels, the recording engineer may be concerned that the setting wasn't conservative enough, and peaks might exceed the available headroom. Under those circumstances, the engineer will slowly and carefully reduce the input level, as needed.

Also, multitrack recording led to outputting tracks through a mixer to a different recorder, and engineers varied the mixer's faders to make parts from individual tracks louder or softer. This practice carries over to today's use of virtual faders in a program's virtual mixing console.

However, technology has improved this kind of manual dynamics control. In the days of tape, if you made a wrong fader move during a mix, you had to re-do the mix (or at least part of it). This limitation inspired the development of *automation*—using computers to record and reproduce fader movements. If you make a mistake, you can edit the data controlling the fader movement rather than record a new mix from scratch.

 See Chapter 4 in this book for more information on automation.

These methods are suited only for relatively slow-paced dynamics changes, because the human hand can't react quickly or accurately enough to be effective on individual phrases or notes. As a result, hardware and software dynamics processors are essential for precise level-altering applications.

Level-Riding Plug-Ins

Plug-ins for computer-based recording setups are now available that automate gain-riding—sort of like a robot mixing engineer who can alter a track's level to compensate for undesired level variations. The software company Waves makes separate plug-ins for vocals and bass for this purpose (Vocal Rider and Bass Rider—see Fig. 1.2). These do automatic gain-riding to keep the vocal or bass at a target level you specify.

Figure 1.2 Waves' Vocal Rider provides automated vocal gain riding.

These automatic level-riding plug-ins write corresponding automation data into your recording software so you can edit the automation manually if needed. Also, many of these plug-ins offer a *sidechain* input, as described in Chapter 3, to allow controlling the track level based on the overall mix's level. The signal being controlled can be louder in louder passages and softer in softer passages.

The main advantage of automatic gain-riding programs compared to other dynamics processors is they don't alter the fidelity or moment-to-moment dynamics, only the overall level. They affect the signal no more than moving a fader. As to their effectiveness, for applications where a consistent voice level is crucial, vocal gain-riding plug-ins can save time. However, their usefulness for music depends on the nature of the music itself. These plug-ins can't make artistic decisions, only technical ones. Fortunately, you can edit the automation if you disagree with the plug-in's decisions.

For narration, automated gain-riding may or may not be suitable. Sung vocals tend to have fairly long, legato notes, whereas narration can have short bursts of dialog. I find vocal gain-riding software works best with singing.

Common Dynamics Processor Parameters

All dynamics processors have many parameters in common. Even though they produce different results, they use similar technologies.

Regarding connections (physical or virtual), dynamics processors have at least an input and output. The processing alters what happens between the input and output. The difference between the input and output signal depends on parameter settings that affect the sound. Although you won't find all of the following parameters on all dynamics processors, each processor will have some subset of these parameters (Fig. 1.3).

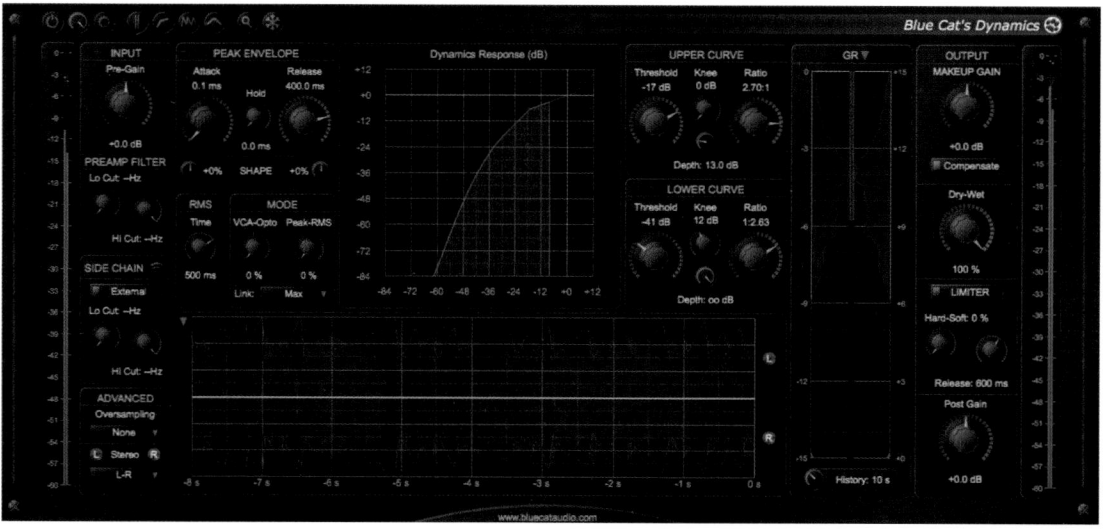

Figure 1.3 Blue Cat's Dynamics plug-in is a general-purpose processor that does compression, expansion, noise gating, and limiting.

Input Level

The input level setting is important because sending more signal into a dynamics processor alters the processor's action. For a given set of dynamics processor settings, the results will be very different if the input signal has a low or high level; we'll discuss why later.

Threshold

This control sets the level above or below which the dynamics processor performs its intended function. Until a signal crosses over (or under) a specified threshold, no processing occurs. There may be more than one threshold if a processor applies different processes to high- and low-level signals.

Ratio

This parameter defines how much the output signal changes for a given change to the input signal. The precise functionality depends on the type of dynamics processing, so we'll cover this in detail for each processor type.

Knee

When a signal crosses the threshold, it's usually processed to the fullest extent of the chosen type of processing. A knee "softens" this action so that the device starts applying its processing somewhat before the signal crosses the threshold, and then applies more processing as the signal moves further past the threshold. Eventually, the full amount of processing occurs.

Ceiling

This setting determines the maximum output level. It's like an output level control, except that it gives a precise indication of the maximum level the processor will provide. For example, if the ceiling is –1 dB, the output will be scaled so that its maximum level doesn't exceed –1 dB.

Output Level (also called Gain or Makeup Gain)

A dynamics processor can change the overall level of a signal. An output level control can compensate for these changes to preserve unity gain through the processor (i.e., the output remains at the same approximate peak level as the input).

Automatic Output Level

This option compensates automatically for level changes due to the dynamics processing. Typically, it sets the level so that a 0 dB signal at the input produces a 0 dB signal at the output.

Mix

This has not been a common compressor control, but that's starting to change. In some compressors, the unprocessed and compressed signals are two parallel paths; this control sets a balance between them. For example, when set halfway, there's still a sense of dynamics from the unprocessed signal, but the compressed signal provides a bigger, more sustained sound. With guitar, you'll hear the initial pluck clearly, but there will also be more string sustain. With drums, the right mix prevents the attack from sounding dull.

Attack

The attack parameter determines how quickly the processor reacts to the input signal when the signal crosses the threshold. Extremely short attack times may lead to distortion; increasing the attack time can eliminate this distortion, and can also give a less artificial sound by allowing a song's natural attack to come through, regardless of the subsequent dynamics processing.

Release (also called Decay)

This sets how long it takes for processing to stop after the signal returns back over the threshold. Like with the attack time, extremely short release times could lead to distortion. A manufacturer may calibrate the release time according to the rate at which the gain changes after a signal crosses the threshold (rather than an absolute amount of time), but musically speaking, you'll adjust this control based on the sound, not the time increment.

Auto Attack and Release

Auto attack and release functions change the corresponding attack and release times based on the incoming audio signal, so the setting is constantly optimizing itself to produce the most transparent attack and release characteristics. With a fully automatic function, the compressor takes control, so these attack and release parameters will not be adjustable.

Adaptive Attack and Release

This is similar to the Auto function, but the attack and/or release controls remain user-adjustable. The adaptive function varies the corresponding times automatically around the set amount.

Hold

This is mostly a feature on noise gates and expanders (described later). After a signal has crossed the threshold, the attack time has elapsed, and any dynamics processing is in play, hold maintains this processing for the set duration—even if the signal crosses the threshold again before the hold time elapses.

Metering

While not a control, metering is important to give visual feedback on what's happening with the processing. Parameters a meter may monitor are:

- Input level, to display the level going into the processor.

- Output level, to show the level coming out of the processor.

- Gain reduction, to provide insight into the processor's actions. A gain-reduction meter works opposite of most meters—the *highest* setting is 0, and the meter moves downward from 0 to reflect the amount of gain reduction being applied.

- True Peak, which takes the possibility of intersample distortion into account (see the Tech Talk sidebar below).

- Histogram, which displays a history of levels. It's usually a bar-graph meter whose vertical axis shows the instantaneous level like a standard meter, while the horizontal axis displays bar widths to show how often a level is present (Fig. 1.4). For example, if the bars are widest around −16 dB, that means the signal hits a level of −16 dB more often than any other level. Typically, the width thins out at the very top and the very bottom, with a bulge in the middle where the levels are most common.

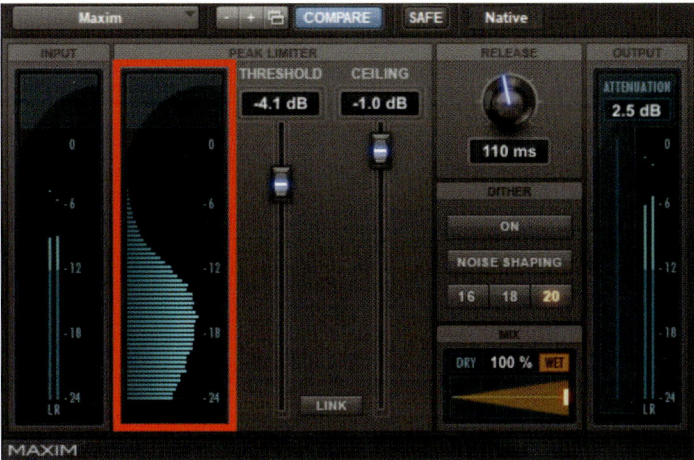

Figure 1.4 The histogram (outlined in red) in Pro Tools' Maxim plug-in shows the distribution of levels, over time, in the song being played.

Tech Talk: Intersample Distortion

This type of distortion can occur on playback if some peaks use up the maximum available headroom in a digital recording, and then these same peaks pass through the digital-to-analog converter's output-smoothing filter to reconstruct the original waveform. This reconstructed waveform might have a higher amplitude than the peak level of the samples, which would cause the waveform to exceed the maximum available headroom (Fig. 1.5).

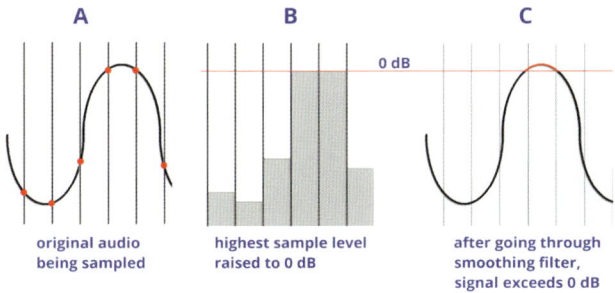

Figure 1.5 With the analog audio waveform sampled in (A), raising the digital audio's level to the maximum available headroom (B) can exceed the maximum headroom when going through the smoothing filter (C) that reconstructs the analog waveform.

Lookahead

When a processor needs to apply dynamics control, ideally any required changes happen instantly. Without lookahead, this isn't possible; the processor has to know a particular condition exists before it can act on it, so there will always be some delay (no matter how small) before the dynamics control kicks in. The lookahead function delays the audio being processed so the processor can analyze the signal in real time and thus be ready to apply processing to the delayed signal as needed. Sometimes the lookahead time is variable.

The tradeoff is that with a multitrack music program, enabling lookahead on a dynamics processor requires delaying the other tracks by an equal amount so that all the tracks sync up. Most modern software programs do this automatically with a process called Plug-In Delay Compensation (PDC). However, you often need to stop the transport after inserting a plug-in with lookahead; the tracks then re-sync upon playback. Although lookahead processing increases latency through the system, the amount of delay may be short enough that it's not a problem.

If latency seems to increase in a project for no apparent reason, you may have inserted a plug-in with lookahead. Even if programs compensate automatically for the increased latency, they may not give a warning that this is happening.

Stereo Link

Linking maintains the stereo image by applying the same amount of processing to both channels, even if only one of them requires processing based on its relationship to the threshold. If the channels aren't linked, then the stereo image can shift if one channel is being processed while the other isn't. When processing stereo signals, you'll probably use the linked mode more often than not. Also note there may be related options, beyond turning linking on/off, like being able to set a particular percentage of linking that preserves some degree of independence for the two channels.

Algorithm

With processors designed for particular types of program material, some algorithms may prioritize fast response, with a potential tradeoff of a slight amount of distortion. One processor might be optimized for complex, musical program material, while another is optimized for speech. Also, some algorithms model the response of particular vintage dynamics processors. These may not be as precise as their digital descendants, but they may have more "character."

Sidechain Controls

These relate to the sidechaining function, which lets one signal control the dynamics of another signal. Chapter 3 describes sidechaining and the associated controls.

Mid-Side Processing

Mid-side processing encodes the traditional left/right stereo signal into two different channels. One contains the audio from the stereo signal's center, while the other contains the audio from the left and right sides. Thus, you can process the sides and center independently. These signals are also decoded in real time, so you can hear the results as a standard left/right stereo signal.

Processing the sides influences the stereo image. For example, suppose you have a drum track with kick in the center and stereo overhead mics that produce a wide stereo image. You can process the kick without affecting the stereo imaging, or process the stereo imaging without affecting the kick. Reducing the level of the sides makes the signal feel more "mono," while reducing the center's level increases the apparent stereo effect.

 Compressing the sides slightly and increasing their level can make the stereo image seem wider, as can increasing the sides' high frequencies somewhat.

Key Takeaways

- Dynamics processors were invented to overcome the dynamic range limitations of playback systems like radio, vinyl, and tape.

- Although today's digital audio technology makes dynamic range limitations almost insignificant, dynamics processors remain valuable as special effects and problem solvers.

- Computers don't have dynamic range limitations, but A/D and D/A converters, as well as preamps, do. Exceeding the available dynamic range headroom can lead to distortion.

- Metering helps monitor whether a signal is exceeding the available amount of headroom.

- The earliest form of dynamics control was a human turning down levels as a signal got louder, and turning up levels as they became softer. This method, called gain-riding, was difficult to do rapidly and consistently. There are now fast, accurate gain-riding plug-ins for some types of audio material.

- Although different dynamics processors perform different functions, many of the controls and parameters have similar functionality. For example, dynamics processors usually have a threshold control; what happens when a signal crosses that threshold varies depending on the processor.

- The input level feeding a dynamics processor will alter the processor's effect.

Chapter 2

Dynamics Processing Devices

Dynamics processors cover a wide range of functions and can be hardware- or software-based. Some modern software dynamics processors model classic hardware versions, while others break new ground and provide functions that would be difficult or perhaps impossible to obtain with hardware.

Software-based processors are typically plug-ins that work in conjunction with virtual recording studio software (e.g., PreSonus Studio One, Ableton Live, Cakewalk by BandLab, MOTU Digital Performer, Acoustica Mixcraft, Steinberg Cubase, MAGIX Samplitude, Propellerhead Software Reason, Avid Pro Tools, Apple Logic, and others). However, some processors can work *stand-alone* within a computer—in other words, they don't need a host program. With a suitable audio interface, a stand-alone software processor can accept the output from a mixer, synthesizer, drum machine, or other sound generator. The output can then feed a PA system, powered speaker, or other sound-producing device.

This chapter covers common dynamics processors. The descriptions follow a similar format:

- ♦ A discussion of background information.
- ♦ A review of specialized parameter implementations. This supplements the previous general control descriptions given in Chapter 1 by describing parameters that have unique or unusual characteristics.
- ♦ Tips on adjusting the parameters.

Limiter

A limiter is like a motor's governor: The threshold sets a maximum permissible level that, within reason, signals can't exceed. As mentioned previously, this was crucial for broadcasting but also could compensate for dynamic range limitations with tape and vinyl.

Limiting leaves signals below the threshold untouched, making it a useful processor for digital recording, where you don't want signals to exceed 0 dB. With the threshold set to a level slightly below 0 (like −1 dB), a limiter can help prevent distortion with light amounts of limiting, and/or reduce peaks to allow for a higher average level (Fig. 2.1).

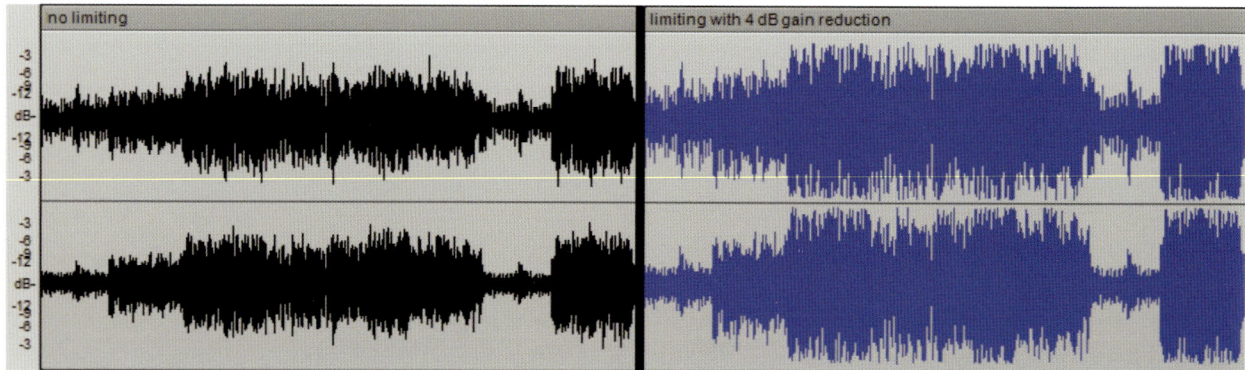

Figure 2.1 The audio on the left (black) hasn't been limited. The copy on the right (blue) has been limited with about 4 dB of gain reduction. Reducing the peaks allows raising the level, which gives a higher average level (note that the waveform in the limited version is "thicker").

For some audio signals, I prefer limiting instead of compression (see next) because the limiting effect can sound more transparent than compression. However, there are two cautions:

- Excessive limiting results in distortion, because you can squash a signal only so much before audible artifacts occur.
- It's important to choose an appropriate limiting algorithm. A *brickwall limiter* exerts dictatorial control over level—it gets its name because when the signal hits the threshold, the level sees a virtual brick wall. A softer limiting action gives a gentler limiting effect, but may allow peaks that exceed the output's headroom, which requires turning down the output level to avoid distortion.

Limiter Parameters and Controls

Most limiters have fairly basic controls (see Fig. 2.2).

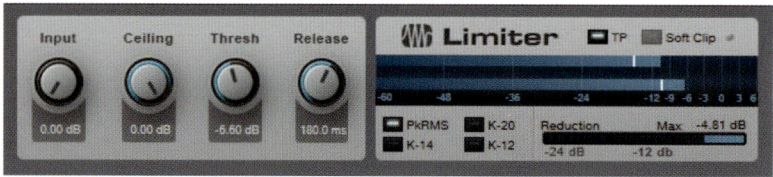

Figure 2.2 This limiter from Studio One is representative of limiters in general. The TP (true peak) switch causes the metering to take intersample distortion into account.

Input Level

Sending more signal into a limiter causes more of the signal to be limited. Although many limiters have a threshold control to set the amount of limiting, some older limiters (and software emulations of them) have a fixed threshold. Increasing the input signal level increases the amount of gain reduction because as the signal level increases, it exceeds the threshold sooner.

Attack

This setting determines how long it takes for limiting to occur after the limiter senses that audio has exceeded the threshold. Higher attack times retain more of a sense of dynamics by letting through initial peaks; however, these peaks will not be subject to limiting, so they may exceed the output's headroom. A lookahead function is particularly valuable when controlling attack times

With no attack time, a low-frequency signal may criss-cross the threshold on individual cycles of a waveform, which results in distortion. Increasing the attack time so that it's longer than a waveform's cycle minimizes this problem. For example, at 100 Hz, a waveform's cycle is 10 ms. So, you need an attack time at least longer than 10 ms to make sure the limiting is not triggering on individual waveform cycles.

 You may sometimes want a very short attack time, to make sure the limiter catches any transients. In this case, lengthening the release time—so that the attack "grabs" a signal rapidly, but releases it slowly—can also minimize distortion.

Release (Decay)

Once a signal drops below the threshold, the release control sets how long it takes for the limiting action to slow down and stop. While it might seem you'd want limiting to stop immediately, this can produce a choppy effect as the signal goes in and out of a limited state. Also, as with attack times, it's possible that a signal will criss-cross the threshold.

Increasing the release time gives a smoother sound; however, too long a release time can cause the limiter to react too slowly to level changes. Typical release times for program material are in the 100 to 300 ms range.

 Short release times with drums can add an interesting kind of percussive, breathing effect.

Soft Clip

This function limits the peaks by shaving off the top of the peaks, which causes mild distortion. Soft clipping resembles what happens with tape when you send in more signal than the tape can handle (Fig. 2.3). With small amounts of soft clipping, you may not notice any distortion.

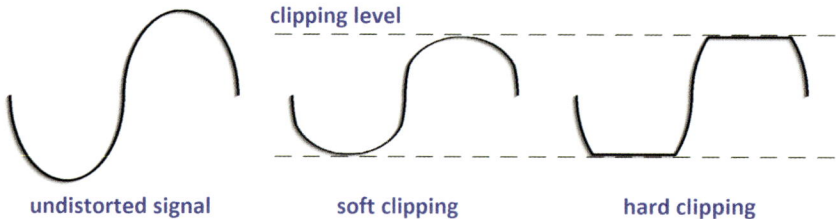

Figure 2.3 There's not enough headroom for the undistorted signal, so it's being subjected to soft or hard clipping.

While it might seem crazy to add mild distortion intentionally, this can increase the average level by a bit more than with limiting that doesn't add distortion. Perhaps surprisingly, it can even make for a more natural sound with some audio source material.

Gain Reduction Metering

In addition to input and output metering, gain reduction metering is important because it indicates how much the audio is being turned down to keep a signal under the threshold. For example, if the threshold is 0 and the input signal is 6 dB above the threshold, then the gain reduction meter will show −6 dB. Higher amounts of gain reduction risk creating sonic artifacts or distortion. Assuming an input signal that reaches an input level of 0 dB on peaks, gain reduction of −6 dB usually produces sonically acceptable results. But you can often stretch this to −10 dB (or even more) if needed, without having an audibly negative impact on the sound (Fig. 2.4).

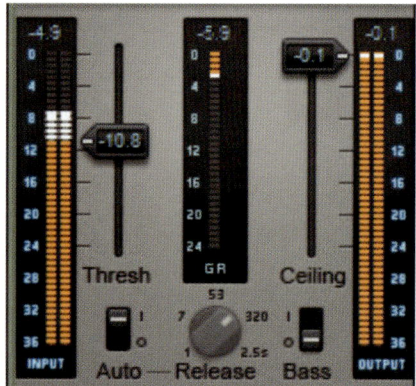

Figure 2.4 The GR (gain reduction) meter in the center is showing −5.9 dB of gain reduction.

Stereo Link

When limiting stereo program material, it's often best to link the channels. However, you'll need to decide on a case-by-case basis whether to link stereo for individual instruments; with a stereo-miked piano, or drum overhead mics, you might want a subtle stereo image shift. Limiters that allow a percentage of linking are particularly handy for individual instruments.

Level Linking and Automatic Gain Adjustments

Some limiters link the amount of limiting with the output gain, so that if there's −6 dB of gain reduction, the output gain control will add 6 dB of gain to compensate. Others provide an automatic gain adjustment so that the output level hits a specified ceiling, without requiring you to make output level adjustments.

Algorithm

Different software limiters use different signal detection algorithms, which influences the limiting action. For example, although responding quickly to transients minimizes unnatural volume changes, too fast a response can cause distortion, particularly at lower frequencies. Multiband-based designs (described later) address these issues, but conventional designs may offer different limiting algorithms: one that's optimized for the quickest response and another that's optimized for the smoothest sound. Some limiters allow separate control over the stereo independence for transients and sustained portions (Fig. 2.5).

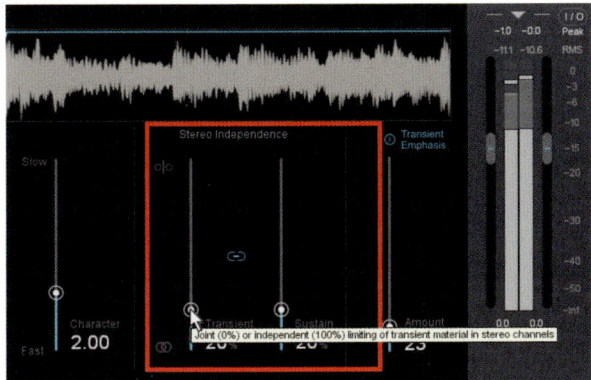

Figure 2.5 iZotope Ozone's limiter has separate sliders to determine the degree to which transients and sustained sounds are linked or independent.

How to Adjust the Parameters

Assuming that the limiter sets the limiting amount with a threshold control, and not by adjusting the input level:

1. Start with the input and output controls set for unity gain through the limiter.

2. Reduce the threshold control slowly while observing the gain reduction meter. Listen to how the sound changes as you reduce the threshold.

3. Once the gain reduction reaches a certain amount, you'll hear artifacts or distortion. Set the threshold for the best tradeoff between the desired output level and sound quality.

4. Set the release control to auto-release, if available. This will usually give the best results. Otherwise, adjust the release control so it's long enough to avoid a choppy sound, but short enough that there are no objectionable volume variations during the release time.

5. Similarly, adjust the attack time (if present) to taste. A longer attack time gives a more natural sounding attack, but the tradeoff is the possibility of transients at the output that aren't limited.

6. If limiting causes the output signal to drop, increase the output level. If the limiter compensates automatically for reduced output, set the ceiling control for the maximum desired output—for example, −1.5 dB to give 1.5 dB of headroom.

With True Peak metering that measures intersample distortion, you'll want a headroom value at 0 or below. This may or may not correlate to the amount of headroom without True Peak metering.

If you're happy with the sound, move on. However, it's likely you'll re-tweak some of the parameters as the mix develops. When mixing, few parameters are entirely "set and forget."

Parameter Adjustment Tips

Limiters have many uses besides clamping peaks to avoid exceeding a specific output level:

- With vocals, placing a limiter with a relatively high threshold before compression (see next) brings peaks under control. This allows compressors to work more efficiently.

- With drums, lowering the threshold can help bring up room sound and wrap the drums with ambiance. Compressors can provide a similar effect, but limiters are arguably better at preserving a drum's sonic character.

- If a synthesizer has a preset with a highly resonant filter, placing a limiter with a high threshold after the synthesizer will keep the filter from overloading subsequent changes when notes coincide with the filter's resonant frequency.

Some audio interfaces include built-in limiting or compression, but this is usually after the A/D converters, which have already converted the signal to digital. So, any limiting or compression can't prevent analog signals from overloading the A/D converter's input.

Compressor

A compressor evens out dynamic range variations by attenuating loud signals progressively to make them softer. This reduces the level difference between soft and loud signals and increases the sustain of instruments with a decay (e.g., plucked instruments, piano, marimba, bells, etc.). Whereas limiting is usually about problem-solving, compression is often used as an effect—sometimes even to the point of being audible as a "special effect."

Compression lowers a signal's peaks. Because this opens up enough headroom to increase the level, compression can also amplify lower-level signals. For example, suppose some peaks reach 0 dB, and compression manages to reduce those peaks by –5 dB, so the loudest peaks reach no higher than –5 dB. If you now turn up the signal's overall level by +5 dB, the peaks once again hit 0 dB. You've been able to add +5 dB to the overall signal level simply by reducing the peaks.

Unlike a limiter, a compressor usually provides much more control over dynamics after the signal exceeds the threshold. Among other options, you can adjust whether the audio has a faster or slower transition into a compressed state, and set the rate at which gain reduction occurs.

Compressor Parameters

All compressors have much in common; if you learn one, you're close to learning them all (Fig. 2.6). For this discussion, we'll concentrate on the musical implications of these parameters and how they relate to recording and mixing.

Figure 2.6 Several compressors, clockwise from top: Softube VC 160, Waves V-Comp, Nomad Factory FA-770, Universal Audio LA-2A, and Softube VC 76.

A compressor can alter dynamics in many ways. For example, Figure 2.7 shows how a compressor can create radically different guitar sustain characteristics by changing parameter values.

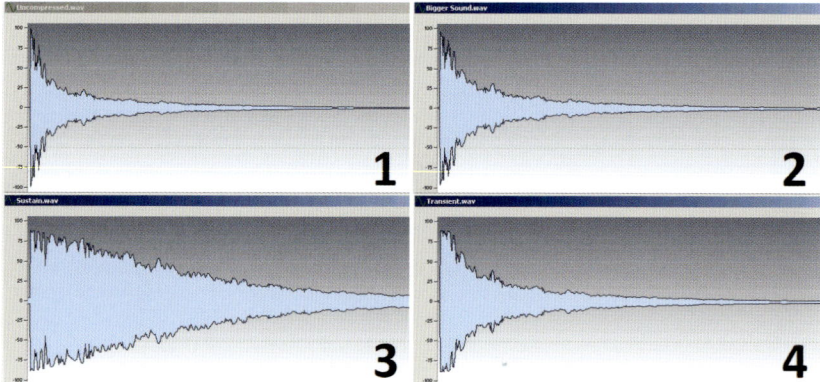

Figure 2.7 (1) shows an uncompressed, decaying guitar string. (2) shows how moderate compression increases the sound's level. (3) uses extreme amounts of compression to increase sustain, while (4) has flattened the initial transients at the waveform's beginning, and has a higher average level than (2).

Input

As with limiting, sending more level into the compressor increases the amount of compression, because the audio exceeds the threshold more often. However, unless the compressor uses the Input control to set the compression amount (e.g., the VC 76 in Fig. 2.6), you'll often set the input for unity gain.

 When creating presets for compressors, try to do so with a consistent input level, and adjust the input levels appropriately when using those presets.

Threshold

This control sets the level at which compression begins. Above this level, the output increases at a lesser rate than a corresponding input change. Lower thresholds provide more compression.

Ratio

This parameter defines how much the output signal changes for a given input signal change. For example, with 2:1 compression, a 2 dB increase above the threshold yields a 1 dB increase at the output. With 4:1 compression, an 4 dB increase above the threshold creates a 1 dB increase at the output. Higher ratios increase the effect of compression, and tend to sound less natural.

Some compressors provide an "infinite" compression ratio, where the output won't exceed a certain level, no matter how much you pump up the input. This provides the same function as a limiter. Also, many engineers consider compression ratios of 20:1 or more as essentially turning the compressor into a limiter.

Knee

Rather than switching instantly at the threshold from no compression to the full compression ratio, the knee parameter rounds off the compression curve. The higher the signal level is above the threshold, the more the compression ratio increases (the ratio actually starts rounding off a bit before hitting the threshold). In other words, the higher the signal goes above the threshold, the steeper the compression ratio until it reaches the specified ratio (Fig. 2.8).

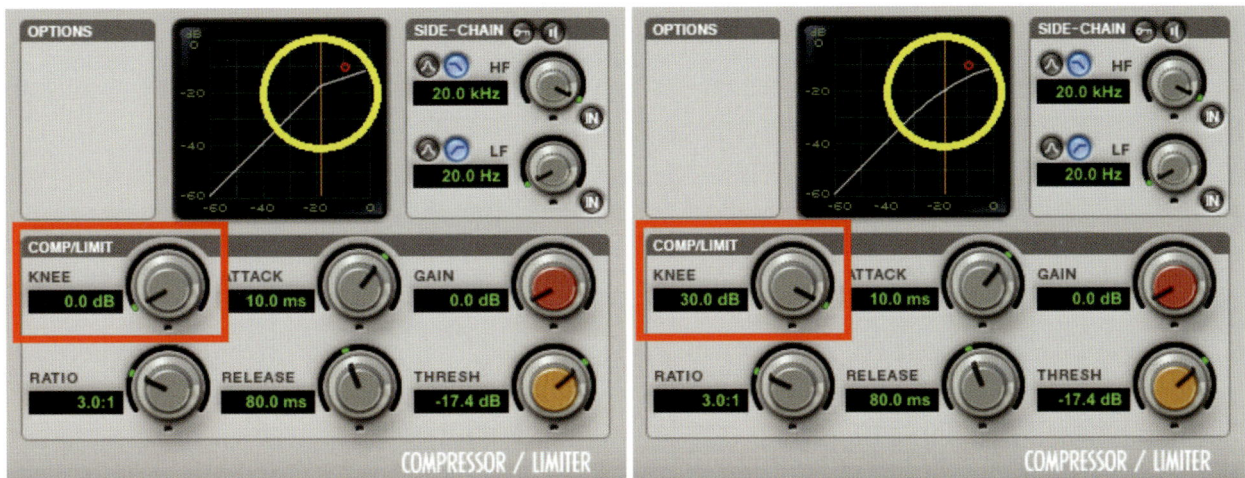

Figure 2.8 The Pro Tools Dyn3 Compressor/Limiter. The image on the left shows a hard knee (circled in yellow); the image on the right shows a softer knee.

Rounding off the curve produces a subjectively smoother sound and can reduce distortion that sometimes occurs as the compressor transitions from no compression to full compression.

Also note that the graph in Fig. 2.8 is a common way of representing compression characteristics visually. The horizontal axis along the bottom shows the input level, while the vertical axis along the side shows the output level. The curve indicates that beyond the threshold (the brown vertical line), the level increases at a slower rate than the input. The small red dot toward the upper right represents the input and output levels at any given moment. Based on the graph, the input and output levels were around −10 dB when this screenshot was taken.

 Don't overlook the knee parameter's usefulness. A softer knee tends to give a less artificial sound, while a harder knee clamps down on the dynamics more quickly and prolongs sustain.

Attack

A compressor doesn't have to react instantly. The attack control sets how long it takes for the compressor to start processing the signal once the input level exceeds the threshold. Longer attack times let more of a signal's natural dynamics through—but remember, those signals aren't being compressed. As with limiters, the same caution applies about fast attack settings potentially leading to distortion. The release (decay) parameter works as described previously for limiters.

Some engineers use a fair amount of attack time (40 to 50 ms) to keep initial transients intact, but then follow the compressor with a limiter to keep transients from overloading subsequent stages. This may produce a more natural sound than either using a limiter by itself or using a short attack time with the compressor.

Output Gain and Gain Reduction Meter

After squashing the peaks with the threshold and ratio controls, the output gain control can compensate for the resulting lower levels. To set the output level, observe the compressor's gain reduction meter. Like a limiter, the highest setting is 0, and applying more reduction moves the meter downward from 0 to display the amount of reduction. You'll generally end up setting the output gain control to a little less than the amount of reduction. For example, if the gain reduction meter shows a maximum of 5 dB of reduction, a rough output gain setting would be around +4 dB.

Detection Algorithm (Peak, RMS, Average)

This isn't a common option. RMS and average algorithms cause the compressor to react to a signal's average level, whereas peak (the most common detection algorithm) causes the compressor to react to a signal's peak levels. RMS and average response can "beef up" sounds that don't have sharp attacks, including program material, vocals, pads, etc. However, this may still let peaks through. Peak mode works well for controlling transients, which makes it appropriate for percussive sounds where you don't want transients to exceed the available headroom.

Type

Different hardware compressors use different methods to compress a signal. For example, tube compressors have an inherently slower response than solid-state types. What engineers often refer to as a "vintage" compressor sound references how tubes compress. When tubes went through a period of scarcity and questionable quality, the search for a replacement technology resulted in FET-based (Field Effect Transistor) units. These solid-state devices have sonic characteristics similar to tubes, but can also respond more rapidly if desired. Another advantage is that transistors don't wear out.

Many modern hardware compressors use VCA (voltage-controlled amplifier) technology, which while very accurate has little of the "character" associated with vintage units. In addition to being sonically accurate, the technology is also relatively inexpensive.

Software compressors aren't restrained by hardware limitations, so some offer a choice of multiple compressor technology emulations. Others emulate a specific technology, or a hybrid of different technologies.

 Different compressor technologies can sound quite different. To hear how these technologies affect a sound, try the various options on different types of signals.

Tech Talk: What Is an Opto Compressor?

Many software compressors emulate the characteristics of older hardware models that were based on optical technology. These units used light-dependent resistors to provide gain control. As the input became louder, it lit a small, incandescent light bulb that became correspondingly brighter. This shined on the light-dependent resistor, reduced the resistance, and altered the gain. This setup produced a different response curve than compressors based on other technologies. Additionally, the photoresistor itself could exhibit a subtle distortion.

Optical compressors have smooth responses, because incandescent lights have a natural attack and decay time as they transition from dark to light and back again.

How to Adjust the Parameters

Assuming that the compressor has a variable threshold control, instead of a fixed threshold that relies on adjusting the input level:

1. Start with the input set to unity gain and the ratio set to 1.5:1.

2. Reduce the threshold level control slowly while observing the gain reduction meter. The greater the amount of gain reduction, the more you'll hear the effects of compression.

3. The threshold and ratio controls interact, so it's difficult to adjust one without also tweaking the other (at least until the desired sound "settles in"). Lower thresholds increase the overall amount of compression, while higher ratios make the compression effect more drastic. Over time, you'll learn which requires adjustment for the desired effect.

4. With lots of gain reduction, the compression will sound more like an effect than a transparent change in dynamics. This may or may not be what you want, so adjust the threshold and ratio parameters accordingly.

5. Set the release and attack controls similarly to how they're set for a limiter (see previous).

6. Increase the output level to compensate for any level loss caused by introducing compression. There may be an auto-gain control that compensates automatically for any volume drop.

 If the compression action is too drastic or obvious, try these three interacting solutions: change the knee to a gentler curve, reduce the ratio, and/or raise the threshold.

Parameter Adjustment Tips

Like any dynamics control, compression is not always transparent. Overcompressing can exhibit what engineers call *pumping* (overreaction to transients) and *breathing* (uneven level variations). One of the more difficult decisions for beginning engineers is how much to compress. Obvious compression effects are often a sign of overcompressing. Unless you're using compression to create an audible effect, you shouldn't really know a signal is compressed until you bypass it, after which you'll note a reduction in punch and apparent level (if not, then you're probably undercompressing). Until you've trained your ears to recognize subtle amounts of compression, keep an eye on the gain reduction meters to avoid overcompressing.

Compression is tricky to set up correctly, but the following tips should help.

- **Start with a conservative gain reduction setting.** Unless you want a "compressed" sound, you usually don't want more than 6 dB of gain reduction. To reduce the amount of gain reduction, either raise the threshold, or reduce the ratio.

- **Vocals get along well with compression.** Compression brings up low-level sounds, so vocals can sound more "human" because you hear mouth noises, breaths, and other elements that add expressiveness. It's not uncommon for vocals to use a higher compression ratio, and lower threshold, than other instruments.

- **For a more natural sound, use lower compression ratios (1.5:1 to 3:1).** Bass typically uses a ratio of around 3:1, voice 2:1 to 10:1—but these are approximations, not rules. To increase guitar sustain, try a ratio in at least the 4:1 to 8:1 range.

- **Attack time settings matter.** A minimum attack time clamps peaks almost instantly, which can sound unnatural. If it's crucial that the signal never hit 0, yet you want high average levels, a limiter is a more suitable processor. For most sounds, an attack time of 3 to 10 ms lets through some peaks for a more natural effect, although you'll need to lower the output level so the peaks don't distort subsequent stages. If distortion is a problem, follow the compressor with a limiter set for a high threshold so that its only role is to catch transients.

- **Release time is not as critical as attack time.** Start with release in the 100 to 250 ms range. Shorter times sound livelier, longer times sound smoother. However, too short a release time can give a choppy effect, while too long a release may homogenize the sound.

- **Reality checks are important.** Toggle the bypass switch frequently to compare the compressed and non-compressed sounds. Match their peak levels closely for the most realistic comparison. Even a little compression may give the desired effect.

- **Place compression early in the signal chain.** When using compression as a track effect, place it early in any signal processing chain so it doesn't bring up noise from preceding effects.

- **Compressors are not miracle workers.** Don't expect a compressor to compensate for dead strings or guitars with poor sustain characteristics.

- **For guitar sustain, add compression before distortion.** This gives a smoother sound, and doesn't bring up noise from the distortion.

- **Check your input levels.** If you experience a sudden increase in compression, but you didn't increase the compression amount, the input signal going to the compressor may have increased.

Compressor Presets: Friend or Foe?

As with so many aspects of audio, the subject of compressor presets polarizes people. The purists say there's no point to presets, because every signal is different, and the same compressor settings will sound very different on different sources. On the other hand, manufacturers offer presets in their products, and you'll find an abundance of advice on the web about typical preset settings. So who's right?

Here, as is also true with so many aspects of audio, the answer is *both*. If a preset works "out of the box," that's luck—it's almost certain you'll need to tweak any settings for optimum results. However, there *are* certain ranges of settings that work well for particular types of signals. In any event, compression depends greatly on the input signal level. If the threshold is set to −10, then signals that peak at 0 will sound very different compared to signals that peak at −10.

The most effective way to approach compression is to decide what effect you want the compression to accomplish, and then adjust the compression settings to produce that effect. Most of the time, I start with a default preset and adjust settings from scratch. However, in some situations (like recording my vocals using a particular mic, for a particular musical genre) a preset will be 90% of the way to where it needs to be. In that case, having a "point of departure" preset saves time.

Also remember that compression isn't some monolithic effect that just "squashes things." Compression can add an entirely different character to drums, because due to a drum's rapid decay, compression can act almost like a transient shaper. With guitar, compression can add sustain for lead parts, or place a strummed acoustic guitar further back in a mix without changing its average level.

 Transient shapers are a type of dynamics processor described later in this chapter.

No preset can read your mind to decide what kind of sound you want. But if you know how a compressor works, you can make it do whatever you want, and you can get there quicker by using a preset as a starting point. So, let's look at some typical compression presets—but be forewarned: you'll probably need to tweak them, which means knowing enough about how compressors work to do so effectively.

Vocals

Gain reduction of 6 dB or so on peaks is a middle-of-the-road value, but vocals can often benefit from heavy compression: raise the ratio to reduce the peaks, lower the threshold to compress more of the vocal, or both.

One way to judge whether these settings are correct is if you can hear every word distinctly. Too high a ratio, or too low a threshold, can "smear" the difference between louder and softer words. If no combination of ratio and threshold seems to work, consider inserting a limiter in front of the compressor to pre-condition the peaks before they hit the compressor.

Setting a fairly smooth knee also helps with vocals, because the compression action becomes heavier at louder levels, which is where you want the most amount of compression (Fig. 2.9). However if the vocalist tends to "spike" on higher peaks, then a sharper knee can control these.

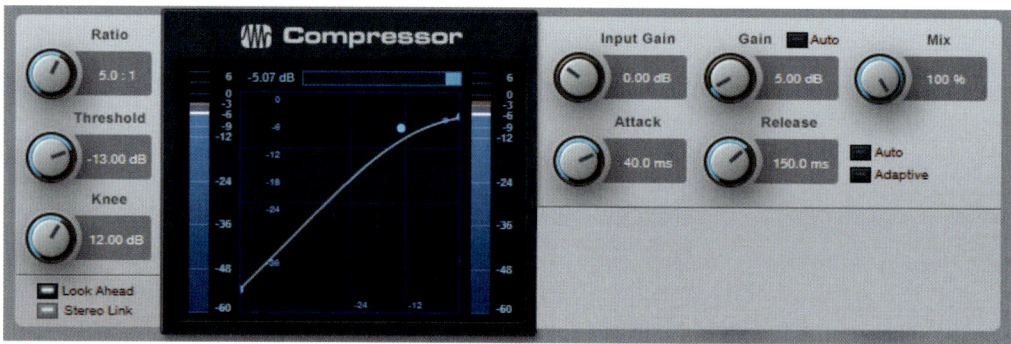

Figure 2.9 Compressed vocals often benefit from a smoother knee.

If you're not using auto or adaptive attack/release settings, add about 40 ms of attack time so that the consonants at the start of words come through clearly. If the consonants seem too prominent, lower the attack time. You'll also need to lower the attack time if the singer hits peaks hard at the beginning of words.

For the release control, use the setting that "tracks" the dynamics to give the most natural sound. For example, with a percussive vocal part (e.g., rap and some hip-hop), a shorter release is necessary to track the percussive quality. For more legato vocals with sustained passages, try a longer release.

Electric Bass

Here's another example that shows why presets need to be modified. With bass, heavy compression is common to even out the volume levels; low frequencies are hard to hear, and the response in amps and rooms can cause response anomalies. So, you'll probably use a high ratio and a relatively low threshold setting (Fig. 2.10).

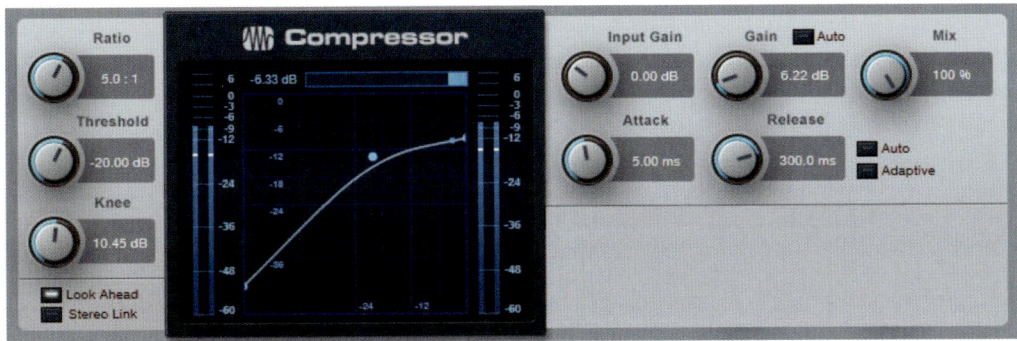

Figure 2.10 A variety of settings work well with electric bass. This one is typical for a more compressed bass sound.

But these settings are not necessarily a given. Some people want the bass to "snap" somewhat, which requires hearing the sound of the compression instead of a more transparent effect. A ratio of 7:1 to 10:1 or more (there are no bass compression police) can do this. Alternatively you can use a lower threshold and a hard knee.

The attack shown provides a smooth bass sound. However, to minimize distortion, you may need to increase this, and for the bass to "pop," you'll need a longer attack—start at 25 ms and increase from there until you get the right attack. Long release times (300 to 500 ms) are common.

Guitar (Sustainer)

Heavy compression (e.g., 20:1 ratio and −35 dB threshold) can add sustain to single-note lead guitar solos. A sharp knee maintains sustain as long as possible, and a short attack time clamps down the attack for a smoother sound. The release time isn't too critical, although this depends on the playing style; a relatively long release (450 ms) usually works best (Fig. 2.11).

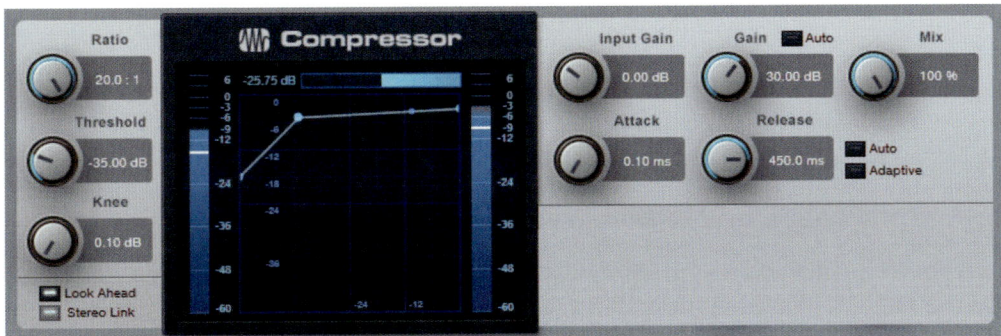

Figure 2.11 A sustainer is a compressor with an extremely high ratio and low threshold.

With a sustainer, you likely don't want to enable auto or adaptive attack/release times. The goal is an effect, not the most natural sound. However, enabling lookahead (if available) helps tame the attack.

Because of the extreme compression, you'll need lots of makeup gain. With these settings, about 30 dB of makeup gain will make up for the gain reduction due to compression.

Guitar (Acoustic Rhythm)

This preset also shows why presets are problematic. An acoustic guitar can play many roles: a fingerpicked, upfront solo guitar; a constant, churning, background rhythm to drive the song; a singer-songwriter's featured instrument; a gypsy jazz rhythm part; and so on. Each role requires different compression settings.

The preset in Figure 2.12 is for an acoustic rhythm guitar, strumming in the background. The settings give a smooth, even sound that doesn't overtake other tracks. The ratio is fairly high to reduce the peaks; lower this for a more percussive effect. The threshold is low enough so that the peaks don't "step on" other instruments.

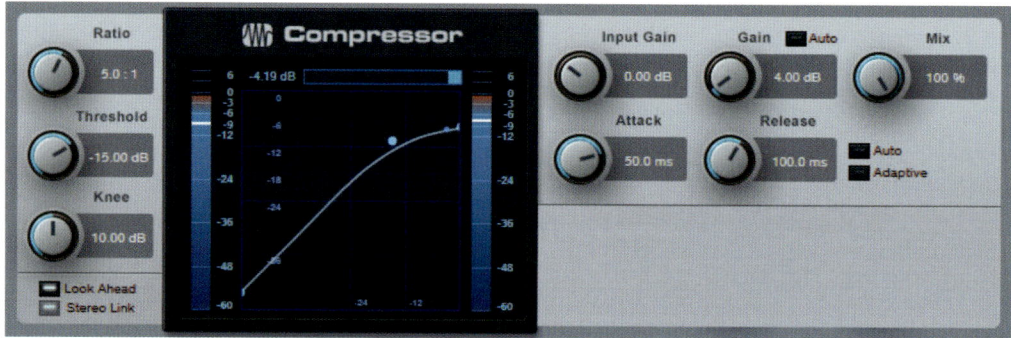

Figure 2.12 This preset applies somewhat aggressive compression to a rhythm guitar that's strumming in the background.

A medium knee smooths the dynamics rather than grabs the peaks. The attack and release times may need major adjustments, depending on your desired sound. In this example, there's enough attack time to prevent neutering the initial peak, and enough release time to track the instrument's strumming. To pick up more of the strumming, increase the attack. For a smoother overall sound, choose more release.

However, you may not want to adjust the attack and release, because in my experience auto and adaptive settings work well with strummed acoustic guitar parts. In this case, the knee parameter takes on increased importance for tailoring the sound.

Kick and Snare

The usual goal for compressing kick drum is an even sound that nonetheless retains punch. However, you have many choices on how to implement that goal. To have the compression take hold rapidly, but not dilute the punch, start with 0 ms attack time. Then, increase it until you hear the initial hit clearly (but don't go past that point). Because a kick decays fast, release can be fast as well (Fig. 2.13).

Dynamics Processing Devices   31

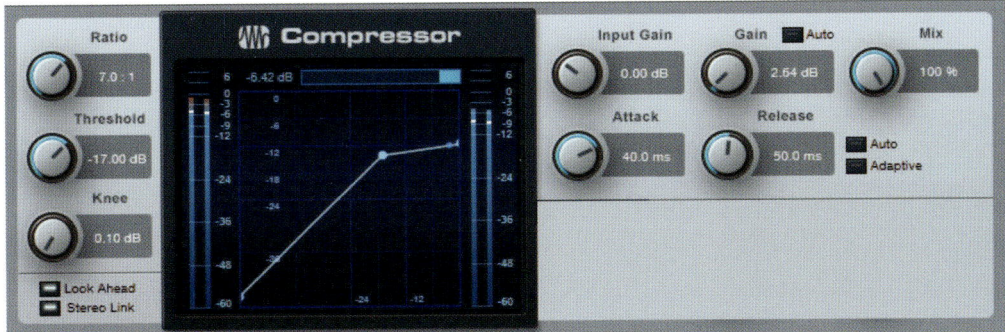

Figure 2.13 This preset is a good starting point for kick (and snare) compression.

Compressors can also do transient shaping with drums. Slowing the attack time softens the attack. Between the attack and ratio controls, you can tailor the kick drum's attack and sustain characteristics, as well as even out the overall sound.

- Raising the ratio increases the sustain and makes space for the attack (assuming an appropriate attack time).
- A higher threshold can emphasize the attack by letting the decay occur naturally.
- Lowering the threshold reduces the level difference between the attack and decay.

Snare responds similarly to kick. However, with an acoustic drum kit, because the kick is more isolated physically from the rest of the kit, compressing the snare may emphasize leakage from other drums. Fortunately, the snare is often a drum part's focus: you can just compress the snare, and accept that leakage is simply part of the deal. With individual, multitracked drums (including electronic drums) where leakage is not a problem, snare and kick still use compression the most.

With snare, a lower ratio (2:1 to 3:1) will give a fuller snare sound. As with the kick, use the attack time to dial in the desired attack characteristics.

With both kick and snare, you'll usually want a hard knee. However, the knee control is a great way to fine-tune the attack—once that's dialed in, you'll have the sound you want.

Cymbals

As with kick and snare, sometimes it seems that compression was invented specifically to alter cymbals. To make the sound more aggressive, set the compressor for a longer attack, lower ratio, and higher threshold. Or, go for a more "liquid" sound (Fig. 2.14).

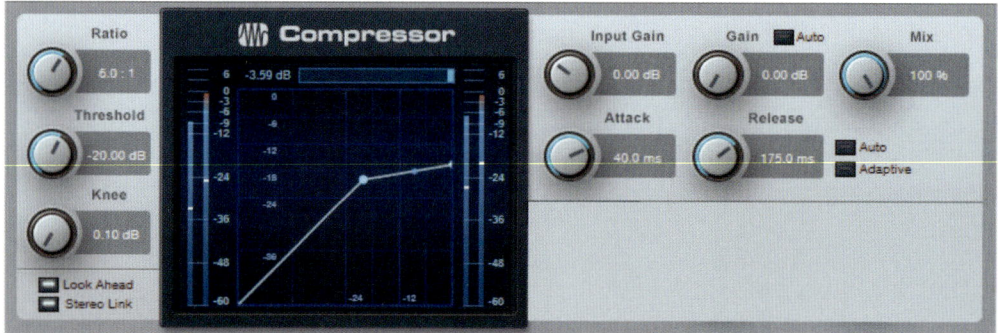

Figure 2.14 This compression preset creates a smooth, pillowy effect.

These settings leave the attack intact, but again like a transient shaper, they affect the decay separately due to the relatively high ratio and low threshold. You'll need a fairly long release time (at least 150 to 200 ms) to preserve the decay. Too short a release can give an annoying "double attack."

Multiband Compressor

With a traditional compressor, a signal that exceeds the threshold reduces the gain and affects all frequencies. For example, if a strong kick drum hits above the threshold, the compression it triggers on a drum mix will likely affect the cymbals and other high-frequency sounds to some degree.

A multiband compressor splits an incoming signal into several bands (typically 3 to 5), similarly to how a graphic equalizer or spectrum analyzer splits a signal into bands. Each band has its own compressor, so compression affects only the associated frequencies (Fig. 2.15). Often, the compressors are general-purpose dynamics processors that can also serve as limiters or expanders.

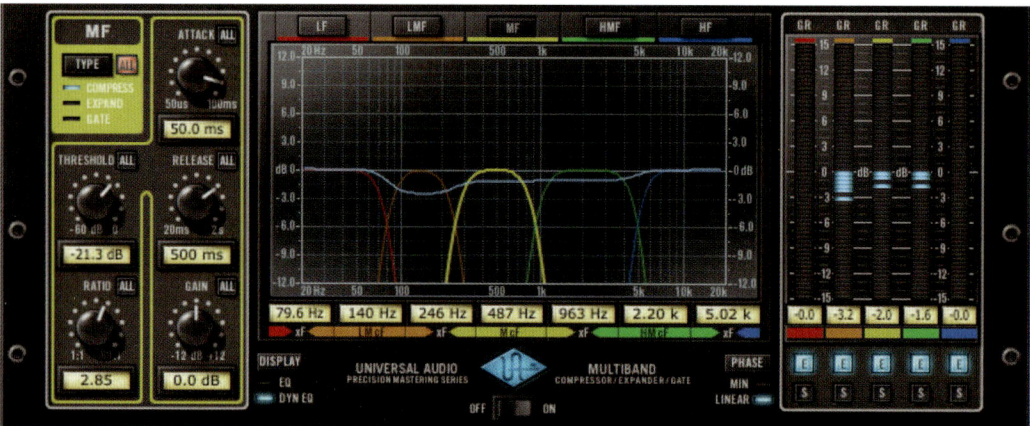

Figure 2.15 In this multiband compressor from Universal Audio, the different-colored "domes" on the graph are particular frequency ranges; the blue line toward the graph's 0 dB axis shows the combined result of all the bands' compression. The meters on the right display the amount of gain reduction within the various bands.

With multiband compression, if the kick drum is in a low-frequency band and the high-hats and cymbals are in a high-frequency band, you can compress the kick drum without affecting the high-hats and cymbals. This gives more transparent dynamics control than single-band compressors. Multiband compression can also provide relatively transparent compression effects for program material.

A multiband compressor can serve as a high-performance graphic equalizer if you set the ratio for all bands to no compression (1.0 or 1:1) and vary the band's level controls. However, it will have fewer bands than most graphic equalizers.

Multiband Compressor Controls

Each band's compressor has standard compressor controls. The only major differences typically involve ways to adjust the same control on all bands simultaneously (e.g., a "select all bands" button for editing) and ways to solo or mute each band so you can hear how compression affects particular bands.

Each band will also have a level control, so a multiband compressor combines some of the characteristics of a graphic equalizer. For example, if you want to compress a drum set's midrange, and not compress the high-hats and cymbals, but have them be more prominent in the mix, multiband compression is ideal. You could apply compression to the midrange, and not apply compression to the high-frequency band(s) where the cymbals are most prominent. Instead, raise the gain (not the compression) a bit in the high-frequency band(s).

How to Adjust the Parameters

Editing a multiband compressor is more complex than optimizing the settings for a single-band compressor, because multiple bands have to be set just right. Think of it like a combination lock: all the tumblers need to be in place to open the lock.

Before touching any knobs, *listen* to the sound and analyze what's needed. Creating a hotter, louder sound is the simplest application: split the signal into bands that divide up the spectrum, and set the compressor parameters similarly. In this case, the multiband compressor acts like a standard compressor, but gives a less obvious sound because of the multiple bands. (This is also a case where being able to edit a parameter in all bands simultaneously is useful.)

Using a multiband compressor to fix response problems can be complicated; the following steps illustrate one possible workflow:

1. Suppose you're mastering a tune that was recorded live. The bass sounds a bit muddy because the kick and floor tom ring too long, the high end is shrill, and the vocals in the midrange sound buried in the mix. You don't want to compress the low end and make the mud louder, nor do you want to emphasize the high end. But you do want to compress the midrange to bring the vocals more to the front. Once you've assessed what you need to do, it's time for step 2.

2. Set the frequency ranges. Most software multiband compressors have adjustable frequency ranges, from narrow to broad, for each compressor. Set the compressors for a 1:1 ratio and high threshold so they don't affect the signal, then solo each band and listen. In our example of a muddy low end, you might omit compression and instead add some expansion to reduce ringing and tighten the percussive nature. Tweak the band's range so that it covers the muddy bass area, but nothing else.

3. Because most multiband compressors have level controls for each band, initially I often treat the device like a graphic EQ. If turning up a band improves the tone but adds too much level, a little compression may be in order. If turning down a band helps, then I generally don't compress it, or use subtle expansion to emphasize peaks more while de-emphasizing lower-level signals.

4. Start editing the compression settings. This is tricky, because anything done to one band affects how you perceive the other bands. For example, if you compress the midrange, the treble and bass will appear weaker. You want to avoid a situation where you bring up the midrange, which makes the bass and treble seem weak, so you compensate for that. I prefer to work on the "problem bands" first: get them right, then complement them by tweaking the other bands. For example, suppose you compress the upper midrange to better articulate voices, or bring out melodic keyboard lines. Once that's set, adjust the bass to support (but not overwhelm) the midrange, then edit the treble to suit.

5. Avoid going over 1.5:1 or 2:1 compression ratio at first, and keep the threshold relatively high, such as −3 to −9 dB. This tames the highest peaks, without affecting much else. Listen after each change, and acclimate your ears to the sound before making additional changes. If your multiband compressor can save presets, save them periodically as temp 1, temp 2, temp 3, etc. That way you can go back to a previous setting if you start to lose your way.

6. After the dynamics are under control, my final tweak is usually to adjust each band's output level for the best overall balance. One of the best features about a sophisticated multiband compressor is that some bands can compress while others expand, and still others can just do nothing—if set for zero compression, they act like bands in a graphic EQ.

Parameter Adjustment Tips

Multiband compression is most useful with complex program material, like a two-track mix, and is a common processor for mastering. However, it's also effective with individual tracks, particularly those that cover a wide frequency range (like drum mixes).

- Bass is one of my favorite multiband compression applications; compress the high end to bring up finger pops and slaps, compress the very low end for a smooth, sustained sound, but leave the lower midrange alone. Chapter 5 covers this application.

- Piano is also a candidate for multiband compression. Leave the low end alone except for very light limiting, so that a good hit in the bass range has strong, prominent dynamics—if you squash the low end too much, the notes will lose drama. But compressing the upper midrange a bit can help melody lines cut through a mix better, and boosting (without compressing) the very highest frequencies (e.g., 8 kHz and above) adds "air."

♦ Drum mixes work well with multiband compression, because each drum tends to have its own slot of the frequency spectrum. A multiband compressor can almost remix a drum part by compressing or boosting certain drums. If you need to tighten up a particular drum's sound, use expansion (if available) to reduce ringing.

♦ Although there are dedicated *de-esser* processors (described later) that reduce the level of "s" sounds with vocals or narration, multiband compressors can also implement de-essing. Focus a band on the high frequencies containing the "s" sounds, then compress only that band. Also adjust the band's level control (if needed) to reduce that band's level further.

Loudness Maximizer

This specialized type of compressor or limiter (preferably with a multiband design) establishes a strict dynamic range ceiling. However, because maximizers are usually intended to put as much level as possible on a master recording, they operate somewhat differently than standard limiters because they need to provide substantial amounts of limiting, yet still sound as natural as possible.

Each band's controls are similar to limiters (Fig. 2.16). Unlike some limiters and compressors that can detect a signal's average level (RMS detection) as well as peaks, usually a maximizer responds only to peaks. Because the goal is to achieve a high signal level, peak levels will be the limiting factor in whether a signal exceeds the available headroom.

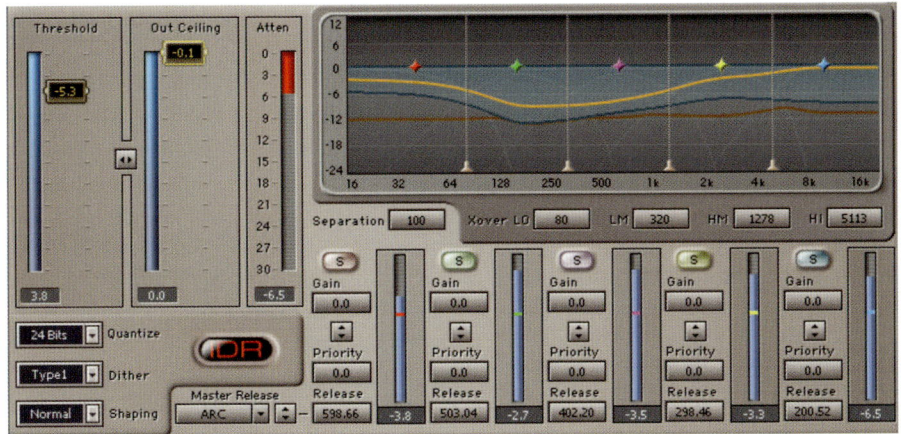

Figure 2.16 The Waves L3 Multimaximizer provides a great degree of control and can boost signals considerably without audible artifacts.

Although used most often with program material, maximizers can work well with individual instruments to bring out a solo from the program material. Select the region containing the solo, then apply a dB or so of maximization (don't add too much). This will lift the solo out of the mix compared to other sections. For individual instruments, maximization generally goes last in the signal chain, excluding any time-delay effects. Processing effects tails can sound unnatural.

The most basic control set would include one control to reduce the dynamic range and another to compensate for the level that's lost. Most of the remaining controls will resemble those of a multiband compressor. You'll also likely be able to edit each band individually. For example, if you're mastering with a maximizer, and the high end seems a little dull, you can increase the amount of maximization (limiting) in that band, or boost its level.

Because a maximizer is intended to be at the end of a processing chain, it may provide the option to include *dithering*. Dithering is a process that adds a controlled type of noise at the low end of the dynamic range, which helps compensate for digital audio's inherent tendency toward distorted sound at extremely low volume levels. Use dithering only in the final processing stage, and only if you are doing a bit-depth reduction for your mix.

For more information on dithering, please see the companion book in this series, "The Musician's Guide to Audio."

How to Adjust the Parameters

To adjust the maximizer parameters, do the following:

1. Set the threshold for the desired loudness. A gain reduction meter will indicate how the threshold setting affects the final output. I rarely use more than 6 dB of gain reduction; more than that can sound unnatural.

2. Adjust the attack and release controls. Faster attack and release times give a more aggressive sound because they're clamping peaks faster and not smoothing out sustained sounds. Also try auto release, if available.

3. The tradeoff for a more aggressive sound is the potential for distortion. Lengthening attack and release times can make the sound gentler while maintaining loudness. Go back and forth among threshold, attack, and release to optimize the sound.

With maximizers, an auto-release control often gives the most natural and transparent sound because it changes the release time based on the incoming signal—faster for quick transients, slower for more sustained material.

Expander

An expander is the opposite of a compressor—instead of *reducing* the dynamic range for *high-level* signals, it *expands* the dynamic range for *low-level* signals—yet it has similar parameters. Below the threshold, the output drops off *faster* than the input. For example with an expansion ratio of 1:2, lowering the input level by 1 dB below the threshold lowers the output level by 2 dB. Expanders are similar to noise gates (see later in this chapter), but are arguably more refined. Some processors combine expansion and gating (Fig. 2.17), much like how compressors may also include limiting.

Figure 2.17 The Nomad Factory Gate Expander 622 has standard expander and gate controls, but also incorporates an internal sidechain (see Chapter 3) that triggers the gate only for audio within a specific frequency range. The Listen button lets you hear the effect of the high-pass and low-pass filters on the sidechain audio.

An expander's most common application is reducing residual, low-level noise. This requires a low threshold (around −45 to −60 dB) with a steep expansion ratio, like 1:4 to 1:10. The effect of the reduction may sound natural enough to eliminate the hiss between vocal phrases, amp noise between guitar licks, and the like without the need for additional manual editing. Expanders can also provide special effects, like hastening an instrument's natural decay, or reducing leakage among drums when recording a drum set.

Expander Parameters

Despite the superficial similarity to compressor parameters, expanders work in a "reversed" way (other than the input control, whose level still has a major influence on the processor's characteristics). Also note that the output control is less relevant, because the peak levels don't change—only the lowest-level signals.

Threshold

This control sets the level at which expansion begins. Above the threshold, output level changes follow input level changes—if the input drops by half, then the output drops by half. Below the threshold, the output level drops off at a faster rate than the input, as determined by the ratio.

Ratio

This parameter defines how much the output signal changes for a given change in the input signal. For example, with a 1:2 expansion ratio, if an input signal below the threshold drops by 3 dB, the output signal will drop by 6 dB. With a 1:4 expansion ratio, the same input signal would drop by 12 dB (i.e., 3:12 = 1:4). Higher ratios increase the expansion effect; very high ratios act like a noise gate.

Attack and Release

The attack control sets how long it takes for the signal's dynamic range to be affected by expansion once the input level goes below the threshold, while release slows down and then stops the expansion action when the signal returns above the threshold. Expansion typically uses relatively short attack times (10 to 30 ms), and moderate release times (100 to 200 ms).

Knee

Some expanders offer a knee parameter. A softer knee makes the dropoff less noticeable—it's like fading in the expansion effect, rather than switching it in.

How to Adjust the Parameters

For this application, we'll assume you want the expander to reduce low-level noise (e.g., preamp hiss, hum on mic lines, the ragged end of a digital reverb tail, and the like).

1. Set the steepest expansion ratio possible, so that any expansion will be noticeable in the following steps.

2. Adjust the threshold so that it's above the low-level sounds you want to attenuate. Because the expansion ratio is steep, you should be able to hear when the low-level sounds disappear.

3. Now, optimize the effect for a natural sound (assuming that's what you want!) by reducing the expansion ratio, so that the lower-level signals fade out more evenly.

4. If the changeover from no expansion to expansion sounds too abrupt, and a knee parameter is available, choose a rounder knee so the signal transitions smoothly from no expansion to expansion (Fig. 2.18).

5. If needed, increase the attack time to delay the onset of expansion as the signal transitions from above the threshold to below the threshold. Similarly, adjust the release (decay) control so that the expander recovers at the desired rate after the signal returns above the threshold.

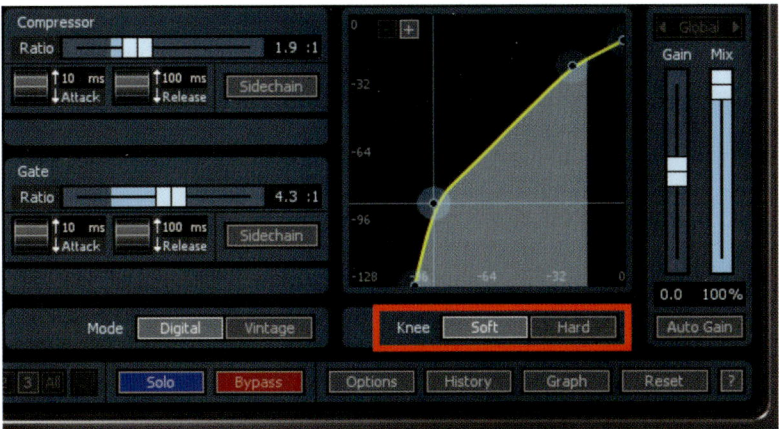

Figure 2.18 The compressor in iZotope Alloy 2 can compress toward the top end of the dynamic range, but also set a second threshold for expansion at the low end of the dynamic range. The soft knee eases the transition into expansion.

An expander can do more than simply quiet low-level noise—like tighten a tom drum's ring. For this application, note that choosing the right amount of expansion requires some fine-tuning, and there will be interaction among the controls.

1. Adjust the threshold to a high setting so that there's little or no expansion effect.
2. Start with a conservative ratio setting, like 1:1.5, and set relatively short attack and release times (20 and 100 ms respectively).
3. Slowly lower the threshold. To shorten the decay evenly, keep the threshold setting fairly high. To preserve some of the initial decay, but accelerate the decay rate shortly thereafter, use a lower threshold setting.
4. If you hear distortion, increase the attack and/or decay times slightly.

Transient Shaper

A transient shaper is a specialized dynamics processor that can emphasize or soften a signal's attack. However, unlike a compressor or limiter, this doesn't necessarily change the overall level. A transient shaper will typically have an attack control where the center position does nothing, rotating clockwise sharpens the attack by amplifying it, and rotating counter-clockwise softens the attack by gradually ramping up to the full level.

Some transient shapers include a sustain control (called Weight in Fig. 2.19) that edits the average level after the initial decay. The result is somewhat like a compressor that separates the initial attack and sustain elements.

Figure 2.19 The PX-64 Percussion Strip (formerly included with Cakewalk Sonar Platinum) includes a transient shaper with sustain, a control to make the decay thinner or fatter, and "color" controls that emphasize or de-emphasize the weight and decay controls' frequency response.

Multiband transient shapers, like Waves' Trans-X Multi, are particularly useful with drums because they can shape the attack of low frequency sounds (like kick) independently of midrange and high-frequency instruments.

Two main cautions apply with transient shapers:

- Unless there's a smooth transition from the attack to the post-attack sound, the two can sound separated. You can usually fix this with proper control adjustments.

- Emphasizing the attack can exceed the available headroom. Native Instruments' Transient Master (Fig. 2.20) includes a limiter at the output to help prevent this.

Figure 2.20 The Transient Master processor (also included in Native Instruments' Komplete software suite) is designed for quick adjustments when mixing. The attack control handles the initial transients. Sustain affects the sound's body.

How to Adjust the Parameters

Transient shaping has many uses for mixing, and because there aren't too many controls, they're fairly easy to adjust.

- Emphasize drum and other percussive attacks so that they stand out in the mix without increasing the signal's overall level.

- Reduce the attack of overly aggressive drums; for example, reducing tom attacks places them further behind the kick and snare.

- Soften the attack of steel-string acoustic guitars if the attack overshadows the guitar sound itself.

- Reduce the attack on electric guitars prior to an amp sim. This reduces the non-tonal "splash" of pick noise that often produces harsh-sounding initial transients.

- Lower a signal's sustain to reduce room sound or reverb effects.

- Increase attack and reduce sustain to bring a sound more to the mix's forefront, or soften the attack to place an instrument more in the background.

- Increase sustain to make sounds seem bigger.

- Emphasize the attack on bass to give more punch. Increase the sustain for a fatter, more even sound.

Noise Gate

A noise gate silences a track's audio when the level drops below the defined threshold and allows the audio to pass through again once the level returns above the threshold. One of the main traditional uses for noise gates was to reduce tape hiss by setting the threshold just above the hiss's level. This effectively muted the signal when it consisted solely of hiss. As soon as a signal was present that was louder than the hiss, the gate would open and pass the signal through. This louder signal would at least partially mask the hiss.

Noise gates are most effective on signals without much noise because the threshold can be set low enough to prevent the gating action from impacting the audio you *want* to hear. For example, a noise gate can help remove mic preamp hiss between vocal phrases or can be used to provide special effects (as described later).

Because a raw gating action can sound unnatural, most noise gates have controls to make the gating transitions less abrupt (Fig. 2.21).

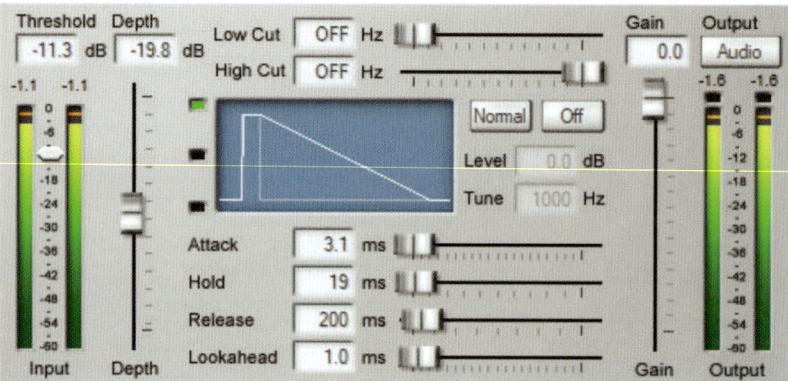

Figure 2.21 Most noise gates offer several controls to modify the gate's action and make the effect less obtrusive.

Noise Gate Parameters

Noise gate parameters have much in common with other dynamics processor parameters, although the way they're used is different.

Threshold

This sets the level where the gate opens and closes. However, some noise gates have separate threshold controls for gate on and gate off. With a high gate-on threshold and a low gate-off threshold, a loud attack opens the gate, while a low off threshold allows the decay to last longer before the gate mutes the signal.

Attack

This control sets the time between when the noise gate detects a signal above the threshold and when the gate actually opens. If you notice a click when the gate opens, try setting a short attack time (0.1 to 5 ms) to reduce or eliminate the click.

Release (or Decay)

After a signal goes below the threshold, the decay time ramps the level down over the specified time to provide a smooth transition from the gate being open to closed. A typical value is 200 ms.

Hold

This complements the attack and release controls. After a signal goes above the threshold, hold keeps the gate open for the specified time. This is useful for signals that cross over the threshold several times when they attack, which can produce a "chattering" effect. Increasing the hold time keeps the gate open if the level drops briefly below the threshold.

Attenuation or Range

Instead of muting the audio completely when the gate closes, this control lets you attenuate the audio by a set amount so the gate doesn't close to full silence. Try an attenuation setting of around −10 dB to cut most of the noise, while retaining a more natural sound: when the gate turns off, there's a less abrupt transition compared to the audio going totally silent. At a maximum attenuation setting of –Inf, no sound will get through the gate.

Lookahead

Lookahead delays the audio going through the gate. This allows the gate to anticipate when a transient will occur and open just before the transient hits. This helps to prevent cutting off the transient's beginning.

Gate Mode

So far, we've discussed standard gate operation. Some gates also offer a ducking mode, which reverses the gate's action so that stronger signals close the gate, which then returns to its open position according to the hold and release times. The most common use for ducking is with a sidechain, to reduce a track's level when a signal is present on a different track.

 Sidechaining is discussed in Chapter 3 of this book.

If you've heard airport background music get quieter while an announcer reports that your connecting flight to Chicago has been delayed by yet *another* hour, you've heard ducking in action. Another example is when a DJ makes an announcement at a party, and the music gets softer during the announcement.

How to Adjust the Parameters

Noise gates can provide dynamics-related functions that go beyond the original goal of reducing or eliminating low-level audio.

- An attack time around 100 ms can cause a signal to "swell" to its maximum level. If you pause briefly between playing notes on an instrument, when a new note exceeds the threshold it will fade in over the specified attack time. This alters the attack characteristics of percussive instruments like piano and guitar, and adds "brass-like" attacks to sustained sounds. You'll find more about this in Chapter 5 on applications for dynamics processing.

- An attack time can reduce vocal breath inhales. A singer breathing in triggers the gate. As the gate fades in, so does the inhale. This makes the breath sound less prominent, but doesn't cut it out completely.

- To cut off the ring from sustaining drum sounds, like toms, set the threshold just above where you want the drums to either cut off (no release time) or fade out over the desired amount of release time. Similarly, a noise gate can help remove the room ambiance "tail" from percussive instruments, and shorten reverb decays.

- ♦ To reduce leakage on a snare track from other drums, try setting the threshold just above the level of the leakage.

- ♦ By cutting off the decay of percussive sounds, so only the peaks play, you can make the sound more percussive. This requires a fairly high threshold.

Dynamic Equalization

This type of equalization doesn't use conventional compression techniques, because it controls an equalizer's boost and cut instead of an amplifier's gain. However, the end result still involves dynamics in a way, and the process of deriving the control signal is similar to how a compressor works.

Dynamic EQ specifies a threshold for a particular frequency range. If the audio in that range exceeds the threshold, then the EQ either boosts or cuts, depending on which option you select (Fig. 2.22).

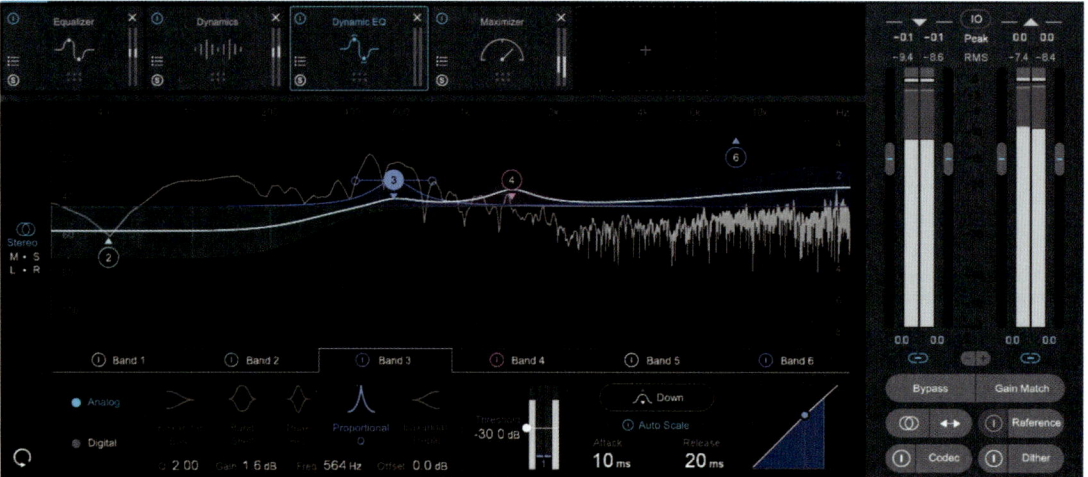

Figure 2.22 The Dynamic EQ module from iZotope's Ozone offers five different EQ types, along with a threshold control for setting when the EQ kicks in.

With a vocalist, you could use a static EQ to boost the "intelligibility" frequencies, but follow this by a stage of dynamic EQ that tames those frequencies if the audio exceeds a certain level. Dynamic EQ is also useful for reducing resonances that aren't a problem at lower levels, but can be annoying if they're too loud. De-essing vocals is another candidate for dynamic equalization.

 De-essing is discussed in Chapter 3 of this book.

Dynamic equalization is more of a tool for mastering and solving problems with specific instruments (like taming an overly-bright hi-hat or synthesizer filter), but can also be useful with individual tracks and sometimes even program material.

Key Takeaways

- Dynamics processors can be hardware- or software-based, but as with other processors, software versions may include functions that would be difficult or impossible to do in hardware.

- A limiter is like a motor's governor—it prevents a signal from exceeding a specified level.

- Compressors even out dynamic range variations by progressively reducing the levels of peaks, which opens up headroom and allows raising a signal's overall level.

- Presets for dynamic range processors are of limited usefulness due to the variable nature of input signals as well as the need to tweak parameters differently for different signal sources. Nonetheless, presets can at least provide a point of departure.

- Multiband compressors split a signal into multiple frequency bands and compress each band individually. Therefore, different frequency ranges can have different amounts of compression or no compression at all.

- If you set a multiband compressor so that it doesn't compress, it's similar to a graphic equalizer, because you can then adjust the levels of different frequency bands.

- Loudness maximizers are specialized types of limiters designed to bring audio up to the highest level possible in order to produce the loudest possible track or master.

- An expander is the opposite of a compressor: instead of reducing the dynamic range for high-level signals, it expands the dynamic range for low-level signals. A common application is reducing noise and hum, as well as tightening up decay times and isolating drum sounds when miking a drum set.

- Transient shapers are specialized dynamics processors that can emphasize or soften a signal's attack. They may also be able to influence the signal's sustain characteristics.

- A noise gate blocks audio that's below a certain level and passes audio above that level. Its main use in analog audio was to minimize tape hiss. It can remove unwanted low-level signals, but it offers creative possibilities too.

- Dynamic equalization combines elements of dynamics control and equalization. Dynamic EQ specifies a threshold for a particular frequency range. If the audio in that range exceeds the threshold, then the EQ either boosts or cuts, depending on which option you select.

Chapter 3
Sidechaining and De-Essing

Usually, the input signal entering a dynamics processor determines the amount of compression, gating, etc. applied by the processor. In other words, the input signal is either above or below a threshold, and this causes the processor to react in a certain way. However some compressors, noise gates, limiters, and other processors include a feature called *sidechaining*. This separates the audio signal going into the processor from the signal that controls the dynamics. The latter becomes the sidechain input (see Fig. 3.1).

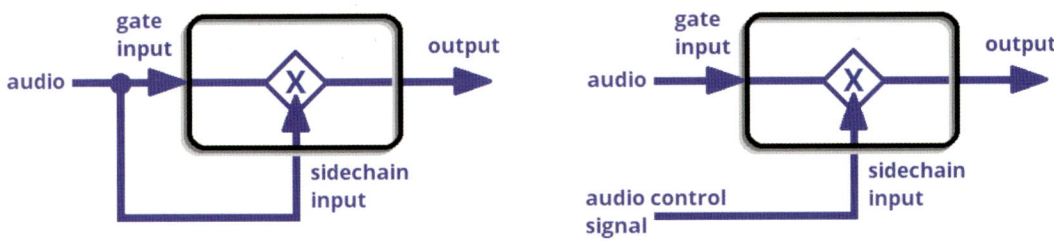

Figure 3.1 The block diagram on the left shows how the input signal controls a noise gate. The diagram on the right diverts the noise gate control to the sidechain input.

Technically speaking, a compressor, limiter, expander, noise gate, etc. is always using a sidechain, because if there's no external sidechain, then the input signal is the "sidechain." However, the term sidechaining generally describes using an external source to control a dynamics processor.

Probably the best way to explain why this can be useful is with two common examples. You'll find more information on sidechaining applications in Chapter 5.

- Suppose you're mixing a singer–songwriter playing live with vocal and guitar. The guitar goes through a compressor, and you want the guitar to get quieter whenever the vocalist sings. To do so, you can split the vocal signal into two paths, and send one to the compressor's sidechain input. A vocal level above the threshold will compress the guitar to create more space for the vocal; when the singer isn't singing, the guitar will return to its uncompressed state.

- When doing narration over a video's music bed, you often want the music's level to dip somewhat during the narration. By inserting a compressor in the music track, and using the narration as the sidechain signal, you can reduce the music bed's level whenever narration occurs.

How to Access the Sidechain Input

With hardware, there will be a jack labeled "sidechain input" or "key input." Software that emulates hardware sidechaining may represent this graphically (Fig. 3.2).

Figure 3.2 Reason, by Propellerhead Software, emulates the hardware connections of physical studios. You can use virtual patch chords to bring signals from other parts of the software into the compressor's sidechain.

With virtual studio software, a processor's sidechain input will appear as an available track output (and/or send), along with other outputs and buses. It may also appear in a specific sidechain category (Fig. 3.3).

Figure 3.3 When choosing an output in Studio One, sidechains are shown in their own category that's separate from other potential outputs.

 It's not always obvious whether a processor has a sidechain input, so check a program's track output options to see if a processor's sidechain input is listed.

Ways to Sidechain

Some aspects of using sidechains require elaboration. As mentioned, a track output can show an available sidechain input and send signal to it. However, you might not want to dedicate the track output solely to feeding a sidechain—to hear the track output, it also needs to feed the master audio bus. Also, most programs will not let a track feed the sidechain input of a processor inserted in that track, because this creates a feedback loop where the processor modifies the track output that feeds the processor's sidechain input.

There are two additional ways to accommodate using sidechains. Each has strengths and limitations.

Duplicate a Track

To hear a track output, and use the same track to drive a sidechain for a processor either on that track or on a different track, duplicate the original track and route the duplicated track's output to the effect's sidechain input. This is a "brute force" method, but it works.

This method also has a benefit that's more difficult to implement in other options: you can modify the track feeding the sidechain. For example, if you don't want a section of the track to feed the sidechain, you can delete that section of audio on the duplicate track. Or, to ensure that the track "slams" the sidechain in a particular section, you can raise the level during that section.

Insert a Send

This is the more common option, and has its own benefits. Place a send on the track that you want to control the sidechain, and assign the send output to the sidechain input. In some programs, you might need to route the send to the sidechain input using an available bus (Fig. 3.4).

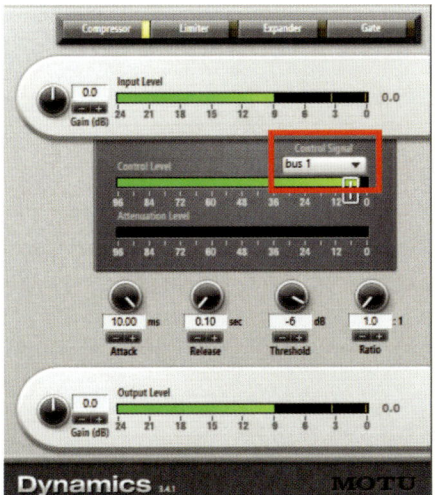

Figure 3.4 With MOTU's Digital Performer, you don't assign a send to a specific sidechain effect, but instead assign the sidechain's control signal input to a specific bus or input (outlined in red).

You can insert signal processors in the send bus to modify the signal feeding the sidechain, and also choose whether the send from the bus is pre- or post-fader. A post-fader setting lets the sidechain track the audio level used for the mix.

Furthermore, because a send bus terminates in the sidechain input, you can feed several tracks into the bus and have them all provide the sidechain input. For example, you might want to gate bass with drums. If the drums are recorded on separate tracks, you can insert a send in the kick drum track, snare track, or any other drum tracks that should affect the sidechain—as well as control the send levels for each track. This means that, for example, the snare could get priority over the kick for controlling the sidechain.

Internal vs. External Sidechaining

So far, we've discussed external sidechaining, where a processor exposes a sidechain input to an external control source. However, some processors allow modifying the processor's internal sidechain path. For example, Studio One's compressor can insert a filter into the internal sidechain (as can many other compressors) to process the input signal (Fig. 3.5).

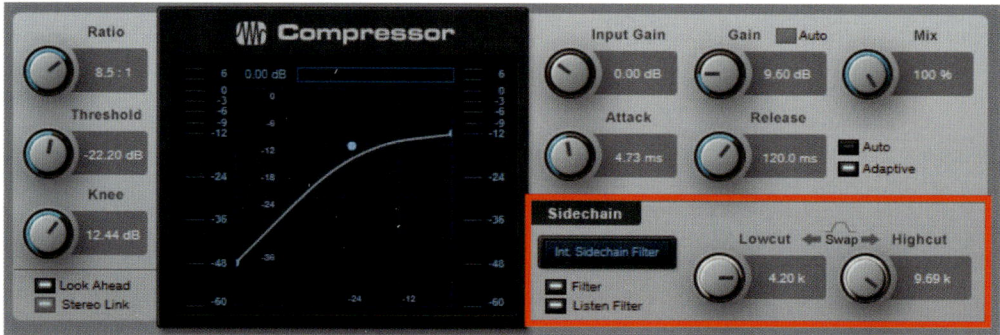

Figure 3.5 Although this compressor has a sidechain input for external signals, you can use filtering to restrict the frequency response of the internal signal controlling the compressor's dynamics.

Typically, there's an option to hear the filtered sound so you can adjust the sidechain filtering. The main application for internal sidechain filtering is to create frequency-selective compression, like filtering out the high frequencies so that only a kick drum triggers compression, or focusing the frequency range for de-essing (see next). With internal sidechaining, the sidechain controls will be limited to selecting the frequency, and listening to the sidechain input. The conventional controls for the compressor handle the threshold, compression ratio, and other compressor parameters.

De-Essing

This is a classic sidechaining technique. While a brighter, more trebly vocal can improve articulation, it can also emphasize "s" sounds in an undesirable way. *De-essing* is a technique used to remove excessive sibilants ("s" sounds) from vocals and narration, which minimizes shrillness.

A de-esser is a special-purpose compressor that affects only high frequencies. This technique requires splitting a vocal into two paths within the de-esser. One goes directly to the compressor input, while the other goes through an EQ to the compressor's sidechain input. If you boost the EQ's treble, higher frequencies will exceed the compressor's threshold more readily than lower frequencies, thus compressing the highs and reducing sibilants.

Most virtual studio software will have a compressor that can provide a de-essing function (Fig. 3.5), a multiband compressor (Fig. 2.15), a dedicated de-esser module (Fig. 3.6), or several of these options. If not, you can add a third-party de-essing plug-in.

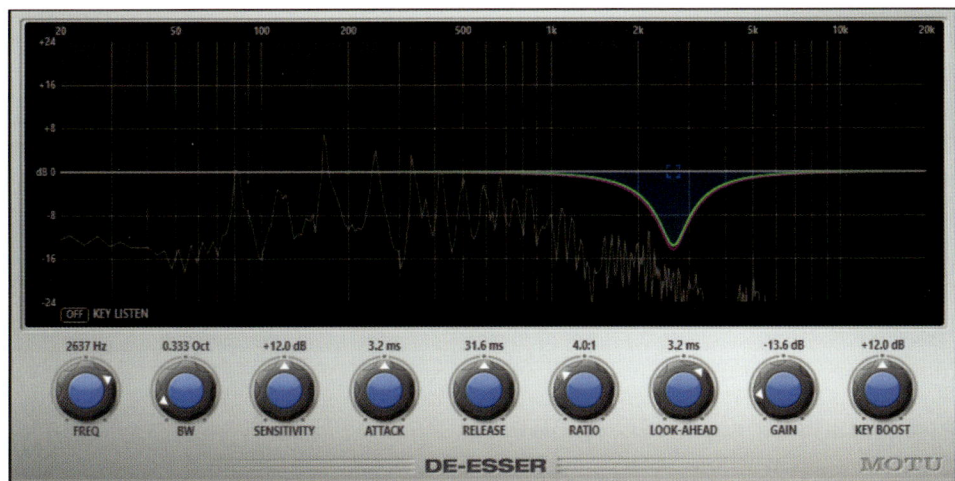

Figure 3.6 MOTU's De-Esser provides a flexible way to provide de-essing for vocals, as well as tailor the treble response of other audio sources.

A multiband compressor or dynamic equalizer can perform de-essing, but a dedicated de-esser will usually take less time to adjust. However, note that de-essers vary in their sophistication. Although some use basic filtering in the sidechain, others use multiband and/or dynamic EQ techniques to de-ess at low as well as high signal levels.

De-Esser Parameters

A de-esser has several parameters that are not common in most sidechain-compatible processors.

Filter

A de-esser requires a way to tune in on the high frequencies that require reduction. This can be a bandpass filter with independent frequency and width controls, or individual high-pass and low-pass filters, so you can vary the frequency range from narrow to broad.

Listen (Key Listen, Audition)

This is typically a switch that lets you monitor only the sidechain signal that provides the control. This makes it easier to dial in the specific frequencies that need reducing. With the listen function enabled, sweep the frequency control until you hear the sound you want to minimize, then adjust the depth control for the desired amount of "ess" reduction (Fig. 3.7). Once you locate the frequency range for the "ess" sounds, you can then turn off the listen function.

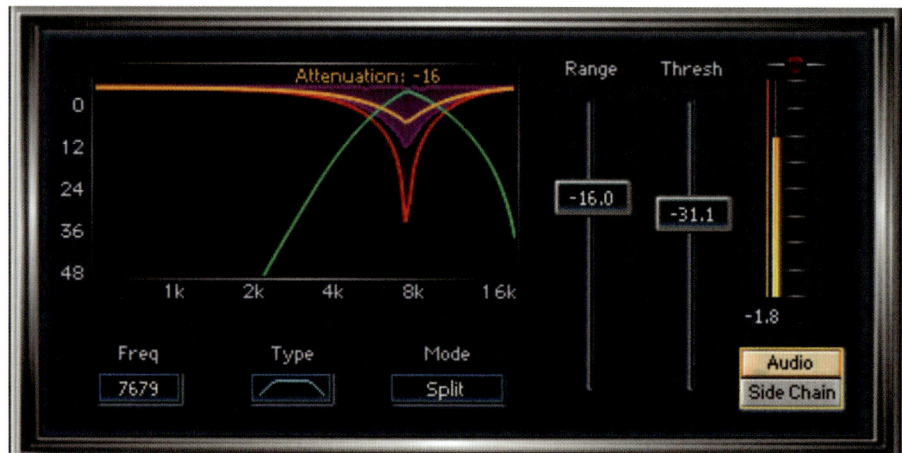

Figure 3.7 The Waves Renaissance De-Esser is set to compress frequencies around 8 kHz. Sidechain monitoring has been turned off, so you'll hear the audio as processed by the de-esser.

Key Takeaways

- Usually, the input signal entering a dynamics processor determines the amount of compression, gating, etc. However, some dynamics processors can separate the audio signal going into the processor from the signal that controls the dynamics, which feeds what's called a sidechain input.

- Technically speaking, a dynamics processor is always using a sidechain, because if there's no external sidechain, then the input signal is the sidechain. However, the term sidechaining generally describes using an external source to control a dynamics processor.

- With virtual studio software, the signal that feeds a sidechain input typically comes from a track output or track send control, although it may come from an external audio source feeding into an audio interface.

- A de-esser is a specialized dynamics processor, based on sidechaining, that affects only high frequencies. It can minimize overly-bright "s" sounds in vocals or narration.

- There are dedicated de-esser processors, but compressors, multiband compressors, and dynamic EQ processors may have de-essing capabilities built in.

Chapter 4

Dynamics Control with DSP

In addition to dedicated dynamics control processors, virtual studio software has DSP (digital signal processing) that can affect dynamics in various ways.

Normalization

Normalization is a basic form of dynamics control. It doesn't alter the dynamics within a given clip, but in its main application, it amplifies the audio within the clip so that the highest peaks attain a certain level. It does this by calculating the difference between an audio file's highest peak and the maximum available headroom (or some other level you specify), then amplifying the audio's overall level by this difference so that its highest peak reaches the maximum desired level. This could be the maximum level possible short of distortion, or a value you specify; for example, −2 dB below maximum (see Fig. 4.1).

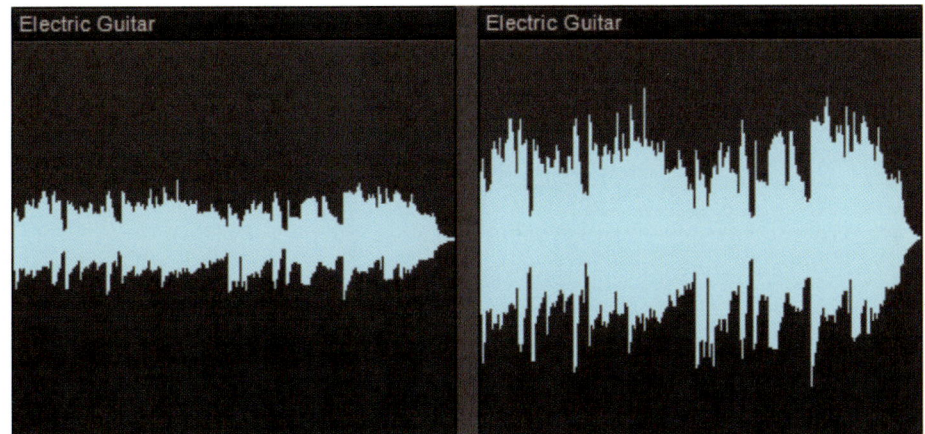

Figure 4.1 The signal on the left hasn't been normalized, and its highest peak reaches around −10 dB. The copy on the right has been normalized so its highest peak reaches −2 dB.

Some normalization algorithms normalize to an *average* signal level, as opposed to peaks. Average levels correlate more closely with how the ear responds to level differences. For example, a dance mix that slams against 0 dB will have a higher average level than a solo acoustic guitar. If you normalize these two signals based on peak levels, the dance mix song will sound much louder than the acoustic guitar. If you normalize based on average levels, their levels will be closer to parity.

Normalizing Individual Tracks on Albums

Normalization has acquired somewhat of a bad reputation because people associate it with normalizing individual songs when assembling an album, which some think will provide a consistent listening experience. Although the idea of consistent levels sounds appealing, this is rarely a successful technique unless the songs have uniform average levels. Otherwise, softer songs don't balance well with louder songs.

It's better to adjust song levels by ear based on what's subjectively pleasing. However, it can be useful to normalize based on average levels as an initial step to bring the songs to the same general loudness. Then, it may be necessary to do only a few tweaks to make the levels consistent, and subjectively sound right. Few virtual studio programs include the option to normalize based on average levels; this is more common with dedicated audio editing programs (Fig. 4.2).

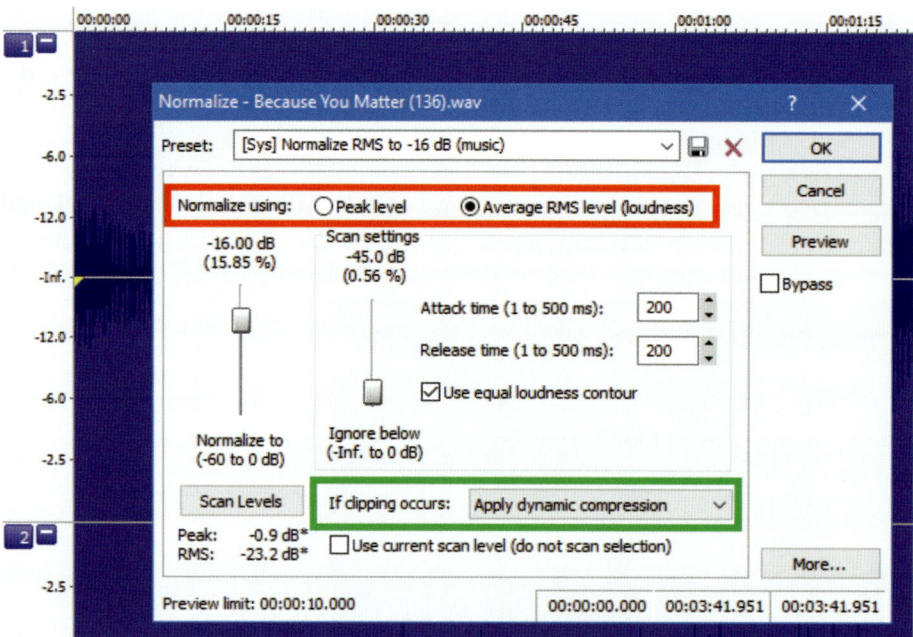

Figure 4.2 MAGIX Sound Forge can normalize audio to peak or average levels (outlined in red), at a level you specify. In this program, if clipping occurs, you can choose to have it apply compression (outlined in green).

Another option is to normalize all songs to the maximum peak value, decide which one sounds the loudest, and match its level by reducing the levels of the other songs until all the songs are subjectively balanced.

Normalizing Comped Instrument or Vocal Parts

Comping's goal is to piece together the best parts of multiple takes (vocals, guitar, etc.) into a single take. This typically involves *loop recording,* which repeats a section of music over and over, allowing you to record another take during each pass. Doing multiple takes without having to stop lets you get comfortable and try different approaches. Once you have multiple versions, you can audition and select the best sections.

However, when auditioning the takes to decide which are best, it's helpful to compare levels that are as similar as possible. After comping a part, I'll normalize each take so that when switching among the different takes for comparison, there aren't jarring level differences.

"Manual Limiting" with Normalization

Limiting can reduce peaks, but it may create artifacts like pumping or breathing. The following manual limiting technique, while time-consuming, is so transparent that it's difficult (or even impossible) to notice it has been applied. Furthermore, if you want additional compression or limiting, it won't be necessary to add as much processing for the same amount of perceived dynamic range reduction. I use this technique when clients want a loud master recording that still retains a sense of dynamics. It's also excellent for narration and spoken word recording.

Most program material will have certain peaks with a significantly higher level than other peaks. The manual limiting process involves isolating those peaks, normalizing them to a lower value, then raising the entire file's level so that it hits a higher peak level.

For example, suppose your audio file's peaks hit –5 dB, but one peak hits 0 dB. You can't raise the file's level, because that one peak would go over 0 dB and create distortion. Instead, you can isolate that peak and normalize it to a maximum level of –5 dB. Now you can raise the level of the entire file by +5 dB without exceeding 0 dB.

Here's the procedure for doing manual limiting:

1. Decide how much level you want to add. 3 dB works well, although as you become more proficient with this technique, you may want to use a higher value.

2. Look for any peaks that exceed –3 dB. Normalize only the peak to –3 dB (Fig. 4.3).

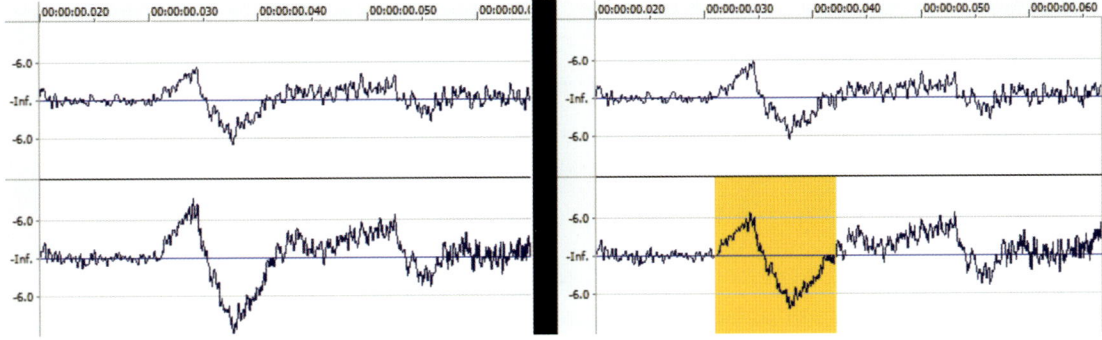

Figure 4.3 The image on the left shows the original peak, while the one on the right shows the peak reduced by 3 dB. Note how this opens up headroom so you can raise the level of the entire file.

3. Go through the file until no peaks exceed –3 dB.

4. Now you can raise the entire file's level by up to +3 dB. Because the peaks are lower, the softer sections can be louder.

 Some programs can locate peaks for you. For example, with Cakewalk by BandLab, you can right-click on a track's peak level indicator (this shows the highest level attained by a peak) and choose Go to Peak.

Because you're changing the gain of individual peaks, which last only a few milliseconds, and not altering the waveform except reducing its level, you don't hear any tell-tale signs of limiting.

Phrase-by-Phrase Normalization

After recording vocals or narration, unless the talent employed exceptional mic technique and voice control, some phrases will be softer than others—not intentionally due to natural dynamics, but as a result of poor mic technique, running out of breath, or not being able to hit certain notes as strongly as others. When relying solely on compression to even out a vocal's peaks, the low-level sections might not be affected very much, whereas the high-level sections could sound "squashed."

To retain more overall dynamics, consider editing the vocal to a consistent level first using phrase-by-phrase normalization (Fig. 4.4) before applying any compression.

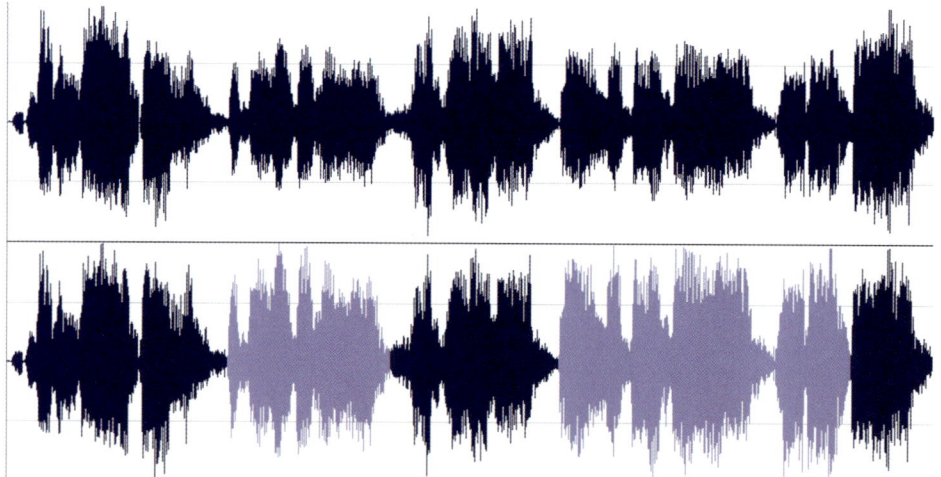

Figure 4.4 The upper waveform is the original waveform; the lower one uses gain changes (highlighted in purple) to raise the level of lower-level phrases.

By normalizing a phrase at a time, you preserve most of the original dynamics, but end up with a stronger part that has a more consistent level. You may want to normalize sections shorter than a phrase if needed, but note that you don't necessarily want to normalize *everything*—some sections are meant to be softer.

When using this technique, it's best to work on a *copy* of the file. After applying any changes, listen critically to make sure the part flows properly. If you hear problems when you listen to the track in context with other tracks, return to the original file to make any needed fixes.

A side benefit of phrase-by-phase normalization is that you can define a region that starts just after an inhale, so the inhale isn't brought up with the rest of the phrase. Also note that if you need to add an element of expressiveness later on that wasn't in the original vocal (e.g., the song gets softer in a particular place, so you need to make the vocal softer), you can do this with automation, as described later in this chapter.

The advantage of adjusting each phrase's level for consistency is that you won't add any side effects from compression or interfere with a phrase's inherent dynamics—even though the sound will be more present and consistent, it will sound natural.

One potential problem can occur if the region you're processing isn't bounded by silence (i.e., when audio continues either before or after the region). An abrupt level change can cause a click where the transition occurs. Some programs introduce automatic, short crossfades when processing a section of the audio, which usually solves this problem. If not, you can split the audio at the region boundaries, and create a crossfade manually between the region and adjacent regions (Fig. 4.5).

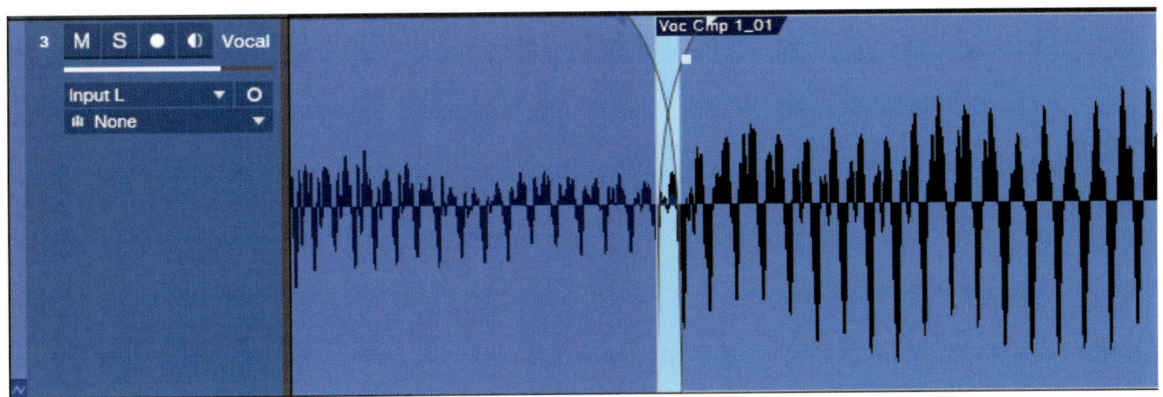

Figure 4.5 The word on the right needed to have a higher level; note the abrupt level change compared to the lower-level word on the left. The split between the two words has a crossfade to smooth out the transition.

Before committing to phrase-by-phrase edits (e.g., by bouncing a track to make the edits permanent), listen to any transitions to make sure there's no click or other discontinuity. In some cases, fading out just before the click and fading in just after the click will solve bad transitions. For these kinds of fades, a concave curve (Fig. 4.6) is usually best.

How to Apply Dynamics Processing

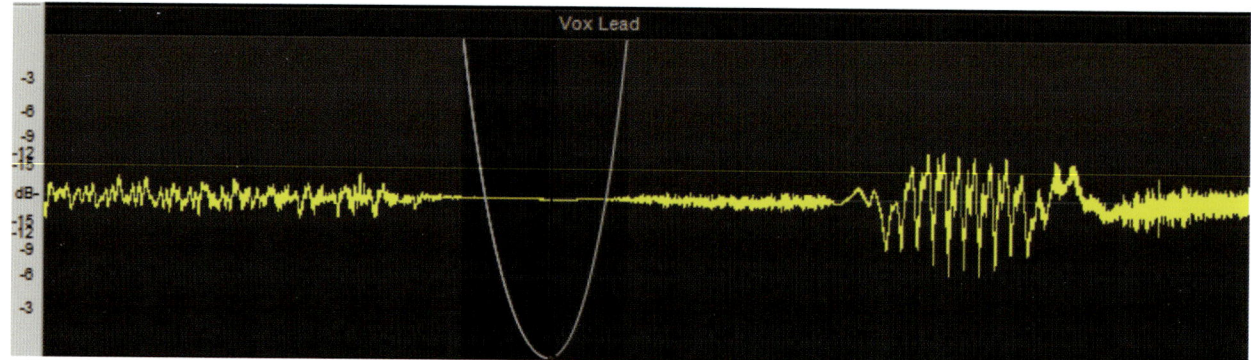

Figure 4.6 Adding very short fade-ins and fade-outs can eliminate clicks due to level variations between clips.

Tech Talk: Phrase-by-Phrase Normalization with Melodyne

Celemony's Melodyne is a popular program for pitch correction, particularly with vocals. Celemony offers several versions; any version above Melodyne Essential can do phrase-by-phrase normalization. Open up the vocal that needs fixing in Melodyne, then choose the Percussive algorithm. In this mode, the "blobs" represent individual words or in some cases, phrases. Grab the Amplitude tool and click on a blob; drag higher to raise the level, or lower to decrease the level. This allows creating a smooth vocal line with consistent levels (Fig. 4.7).

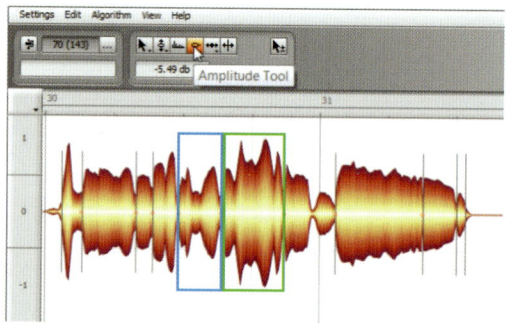

Figure 4.7 Increasing the level of the blob highlighted in blue, and lowering the level of the blob highlighted in green will bring their levels more into line with the rest of the vocal.

For more precise control, you can split blobs with Melodyne's split tool. For example, if just the end of a word needs a level increase, split it off and process it separately. As to cautions, be careful not to increase the levels beyond the available headroom, and be aware that some blobs might represent an inhale or plosive. You don't want to raise those, so listen while you adjust.

Dynamics via Automation

In addition to the dynamics of individual parts, there are more global musical dynamics—crescendos, diminuendos, and the like. Ideally, the players produce these dynamics. But if not, virtual studio software can add dynamic expression when mixing by creating volume variations through *automation.* With automation, if you raise the level of a track's fader to create a crescendo, the program will remember this fader move. When you set a track to read automation, on playback the program will replicate the mixing moves and repeat them every time you play that section of the song.

What You Can Automate

For individual tracks, most programs can automate level, pan, mute, send level, and send pan, as well as track EQ parameters like gain, frequency, Q, filter type, etc. For bus tracks (if present), you typically can automate input level, input pan, output pan, and output level. For dynamics, our main interest is automating level, although automating some processor parameters can also impart dynamics.

MIDI tracks implement automation similarly, but they have a different repertoire of controllable parameters. Volume, pan, mute, reverb, and chorus are common, but you can automate any parameter that responds to MIDI controllers (filter frequency, envelope generator times, tuning, and the like) by creating MIDI automation envelopes that transmit corresponding controller data.

With either MIDI or audio automation, you can edit, overdub, and punch automation data if needed.

 Automation is particularly helpful for adding dynamics to electronic instruments, which tend to have a more static sound than acoustic or electric instruments. Dynamics can help the music come alive.

Automating Signal Processor Parameters

Many dynamics plug-in processors have automatable parameters. As noted previously, a compressor's attack time can have a huge effect on how a kick or snare drum sounds. Automation can (for example) reduce the attack time to make the drum attack less prominent, or lengthen the attack time so that the drum hits harder.

Automation Basics

Dynamics automation can generally be created in one of three ways:

- Moving on-screen controls in real time and recording the motions.
- Creating or editing envelopes that change a parameter value over time.
- Recording data from an external hardware controller.

Recording automation moves is a different process than recording audio or MIDI data. With almost all programs you do not need (or want) the transport to be in record mode, so you can record automation without being concerned about overwriting audio or MIDI data.

Different programs have different ways of arming (or enabling) a parameter for automation, so consult your documentation. One common approach is right-clicking on a control and selecting a context menu choice that specifies arming for automation (Fig. 4.8). Also, many programs have standardized on clicking a W button to write automation and clicking an R button to read automation. Both functions can be on at the same time. New automation overwrites existing automation data.

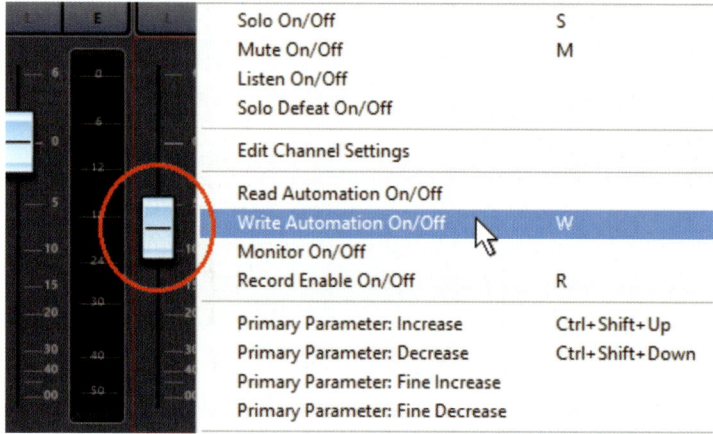

Figure 4.8 Right-click on a level fader in Cubase, then select Write Automation, and the program will remember your fader moves.

Most recording programs represent your automation moves using an *envelope*—a line that traces the automation variations. Automation envelopes can usually be displayed either in their own lanes (these look like a subset of a track; see Fig. 4.9) or superimposed on the track itself (or both).

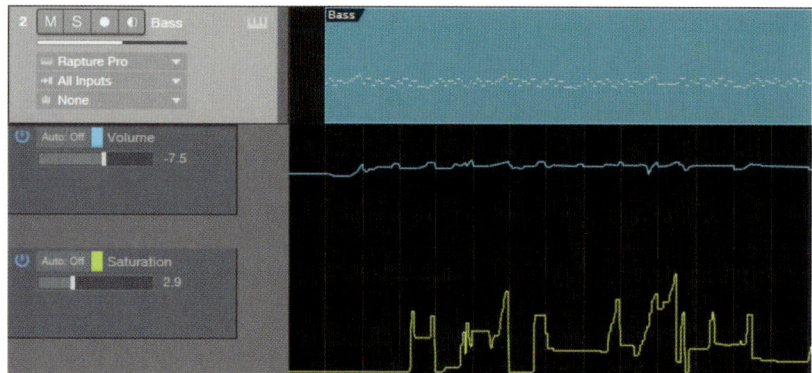

Figure 4.9 Studio One's automation lanes are controlling a bass track's volume as well as a mild saturation effect.

At a project's start, an automation envelope will be a straight line, with its base level set by the fader (or other control) of the parameter being automated. Clicking on this line creates a *node* (a dot representing a specific value at a specific point on the timeline). Dragging the node higher or lower changes the automation value, while dragging the node left or right chooses the position where the automation change takes place. With enough nodes, you can draw very detailed automation moves. Also, you can often alter the shape of the line between nodes to create different curve types (Fig. 4.10).

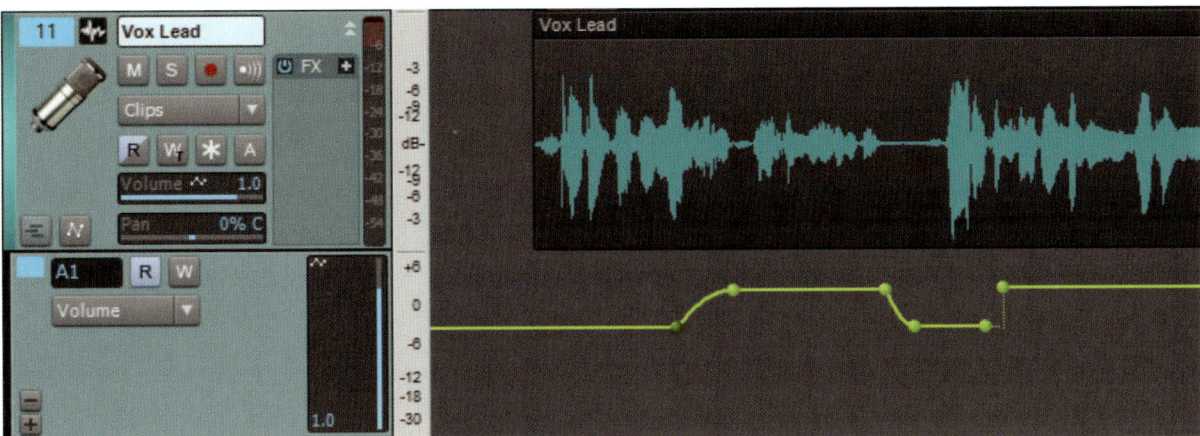

Figure 4.10 This automation data in Cakewalk has curved level changes (or they could be straight lines). Toward the end, a "jump" change raises the level quickly.

Automation Methods

Let's go deeper into the three automation methods mentioned above.

Method 1: Record On-Screen Control Motion

This accommodates the human touch, because you move the fader as desired with your mouse (or with your finger on a touch screen). You can modify these moves later by editing the envelopes these motions create—see Method 2 below. Although you can change only one parameter at a time with a mouse, with a hardware control surface (as described later) you can change multiple parameters simultaneously.

 Some programs offer macro controls, allowing a single control to affect multiple parameters. Using a macro control, you can automate several parameters at once.

Creating automation is similar for most programs. Enable automation recording, and while holding down the mouse button, move the fader (or other parameter via knob, switch, or slider) that you want to control. To stop writing automation, release the mouse button. Any existing automation data then resumes. You can punch in automation over existing automation. Some programs include a *latch* mode so that when you release the mouse button, the current automation value persists instead of reverting to previous automation data.

To resume recording automation moves, click and hold the mouse button again. Because it's so simple to start and stop writing automation, you can "touch up" the automation easily if needed.

Method 2: Draw/Edit Envelopes

Moving an on-screen control while recording automation creates a corresponding automation envelope. You can edit an existing envelope or draw a new one from scratch, as well as show, hide, copy, paste, and perform other automation envelope–related operations.

Because moving controls creates envelopes, and drawing envelopes moves the on-screen controls they affect, these methods are somewhat interchangeable. In addition to creating nodes that specify automation envelope values, most programs have ways to shape the line between nodes.

Method 3: Record Automation Moves from External Control Hardware

When adding dynamics, a control surface provides physical faders, which some people find more satisfying than virtual ones. Using an external hardware controller for automation follows the same basic procedures as recording a control's on-screen motion, because the external hardware controller mirrors the on-screen controls.

After setting up a parameter to respond to an external control signal (see the Tech Talk sidebar), start recording automation and moving the hardware controls. The automation data will appear as an envelope—just as if you'd moved an on-screen fader. If the controller features motorized faders, the faders will move during playback to follow the recorded envelope values.

Tech Talk: Assigning Controls and Using MIDI Learn

Many virtual mixers support either the Mackie Control protocol or the older HUI (Human User Interface) protocol. Mackie- or HUI-compatible control surfaces will automatically "know" which faders and other controls (pan, solo, mute, and the like) to associate with which hardware controllers—they're plug-and-play, once you make your host software aware of the control surface.

Controlling MIDI is a different matter, because different parameters respond to different MIDI controllers. Although some are standardized, that's not a requirement. As a result, the MIDI Learn feature is one of the best inventions ever for those who use hardware controllers. When you select a parameter you want to control and enable MIDI Learn, simply moving a hardware controller completes the assignment process. That controller now provides real time control over the selected parameter.

To initiate MIDI Learn, you usually select this option from a context menu (right-click or command-click on a control). MIDI Learn is very handy with MIDI keyboard controllers that include multiple faders, pads, rotary controls, and the like. Because MIDI Learn happens on a per-project basis, you needn't be overly concerned about consistent control assignments.

An external control surface with motorized faders (see Fig. 4.11) will likely include a feature called *touch faders*. Automation recording begins when you touch the fader and stops when you let go.

Figure 4.11 The PreSonus FaderPort 8 provides eight motorized faders as well as multiple switches. While designed to integrate most effectively with the company's Studio One software, it is both Mackie Control- and HUI-compatible, so it can control parameters in other programs.

Clip Gain Automation

In addition to track envelopes, many programs can automate parameters like level in individual audio clips. This can be the quickest option if you need to make only a few edits for dynamics.

You may be able to place nodes anywhere within the clip, or with simpler methods, have nodes only at the clip's start and end. In some programs (e.g., Pro Tools and Studio One), the waveform graphic changes to reflect any level changes. In other programs, the graphic representation doesn't change, even though the level does.

Ableton Live includes multiple clip editing options for clip-specific parameters (Fig. 4.12), as well as standard mixer-oriented envelopes like level, pan, and send.

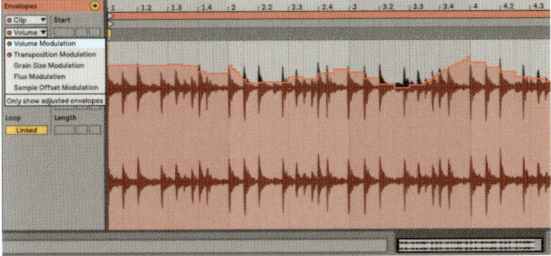

Figure 4.12 This clip envelope in Ableton Live controls volume modulation.

Key Takeaways

- In addition to processors that are dedicated to dynamics control, virtual studio software has DSP (digital signal processing) that can affect dynamics in various ways.

- Normalization is a basic form of dynamics control. It doesn't alter the dynamics within a given clip, but in its main application, amplifies the audio so the clip's highest peaks attain a specified level.

- Normalizing small pieces of audio can do the equivalent of manual limiting, although this can be time-consuming.

- Narration and vocals sometimes benefit from phrase-by-phrase normalization.

- Virtual studio software automation can provide ways to control dynamics by programming changes in levels and signal processor parameters.

- There are several ways to create automation—moving on-screen controls, drawing in automation, and/or recording data from an external hardware controller.

- Automation can control audio and MIDI parameters.

- Automation works with tracks, but can also alter parameters within individual audio clips.

Chapter 5

Dynamics Processor Applications

Processing on the Master Bus

Traditionally, mixing and mastering were separate processes. Mixing's goal was to provide the ideal balance among tracks, while mastering added the final polish to that balance, made sure the mix fit into the target playback medium's dynamic range, and ensured sonic consistency over the course of an album. Mix engineers often did not add processors to the stereo bus when creating a final mixdown, not only out of respect for the mastering engineers' ability to prep a master for vinyl, but because mastering suites usually had the best tools to complement the mixing engineer's expertise.

This tradition continued into the early days of digital recording, for practical as well as aesthetic reasons. Inserting multiple plug-ins in multitrack projects required plug-ins with light CPU consumption, owing to that era's limited computer power. Mastering plug-ins were designed for maximum fidelity and accuracy because you could distribute the computer's power over far fewer plug-ins. So, you would bring the final mixes into programs that were optimized for mastering, like Sound Forge, Wavelab, Samplitude, and others.

Today, mastering engineers specify the type of files they would like to receive. Some are fine with receiving files that already have processors applied to the stereo mix, if the artist feels that it best represents the music. Other artists defer to the mastering engineer's expertise to make those decisions, and some (if not most) mastering engineers prefer the flexibility to do what will benefit the artist's vision the most.

With today's more powerful computers, more musicians are adding mastering-type processors to the master bus (and sometimes even individual tracks). As part of the mixing process, many mixers are doing what they consider mastering. Often, this includes using dynamics processing (Fig. 5.1).

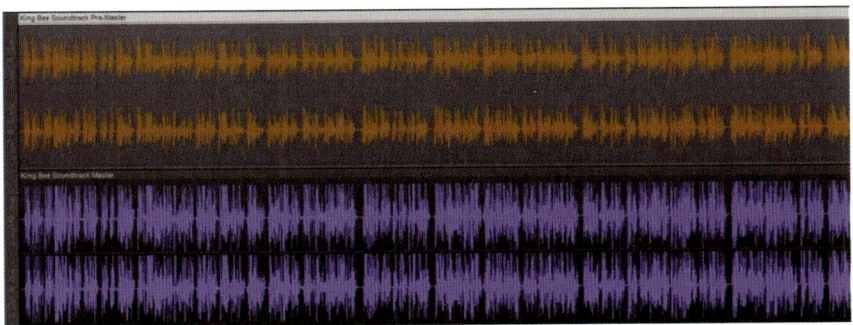

Figure 5.1 The uncompressed pre-master is shown at the top; the compressed version is shown below.

When a mastering engineer's expertise isn't required, this is a valid way to work. (I prefer to treat mixing and mastering as separate processes, even if you're doing both yourself, but to each his own.)

If you do treat mixing and mastering as separate processes, then it's common not to add processors to the master bus. There's a reason to do this, aside from the usual caveat of not tying the mastering engineer's hands. (Incidentally, this isn't just about brickwall limiting; a lot of folks think, "Well I'll add just a little 'glue' to the master bus so the tracks sit together better," but even that can impact what we're about to cover.)

Why You May Not Want to Compress the Master Bus When Mixing

For me, mastering is primarily about EQ and to a lesser extent, dynamics. However, EQ before or after dynamics produces different results. For example, if you want to make an EDM track's kick drum louder during the mastering process and insert EQ after limiting, the kick will sound big—but the higher level will exceed the threshold the limiter imposed. If this exceeds the available headroom, you'll need to lower the overall level.

If the EQ is before limiting, then you're "pushing" the kick into the limiter. This won't increase the post-limiter level, but gives the psycho-acoustic sense of more kick. The music sounds like it's straining a little more, and has an added feeling of power. This is especially true with stereo compression, as opposed to multiband compression.

Some situations are the reverse. If a mix needs to be brighter, I may add that processing post-dynamics so that the extra treble doesn't get compressed, and adjust the level to make sure the available headroom isn't being exceeded.

Although processing the master bus while mixing is a valid technique, there's an equally valid reason to create pre-masters without master bus processing, and then apply processing as needed while mastering to produce the final stereo (or surround) master. This is especially true when songs are mixed by different engineers in different studios, or when they come from different sources and are destined for a compilation album.

Multiband Dynamics for Bass

I'm not a fan of super-heavy compression, but I sometimes make an exception for bass. Mics, speakers, and rooms tend to have the most response anomalies in their bass ranges. Even if you're recording bass directly into an audio interface or mixer, compression can help even out the response for a smoother, rounder sound.

Although single-band compressors are the usual choice for bass, a multiband dynamics processor can serve simultaneously as a compressor and graphic EQ. Typically, I'll apply a lot of compression to the lowest band (with the low band's crossover frequency set below about 200 Hz), light compression to the low-mid bands, and medium compression to the high-mid band (from about 1.2 kHz to 6 kHz). I often trim the level a bit for the low-mid bands, and for the band above 5 to 6 kHz because there's not a lot of energy up there with bass. Another advantage of multiband dynamics is that you can tweak the high and low band gain parameters to alter the levels, so that the bass fits well with the rest of the tracks, without using additional EQ processing (unless you need more detailed equalization).

 If a multiband compressor can also do expansion, try setting a ratio below 1.0 for the highest band so that it turns into an expander. This can reduce any hiss that's present in the very highest band.

The preset in Fig. 5.2 gives a sound like "tuned thunder," thanks to heavy compression in the lowest band. Start from a default setting where the band crossover frequencies are 125, 320, 1,200 and 4,000 Hz, with thresholds of −12 dB, ratios of 2:1, slight knees, and auto response for the attack and release controls.

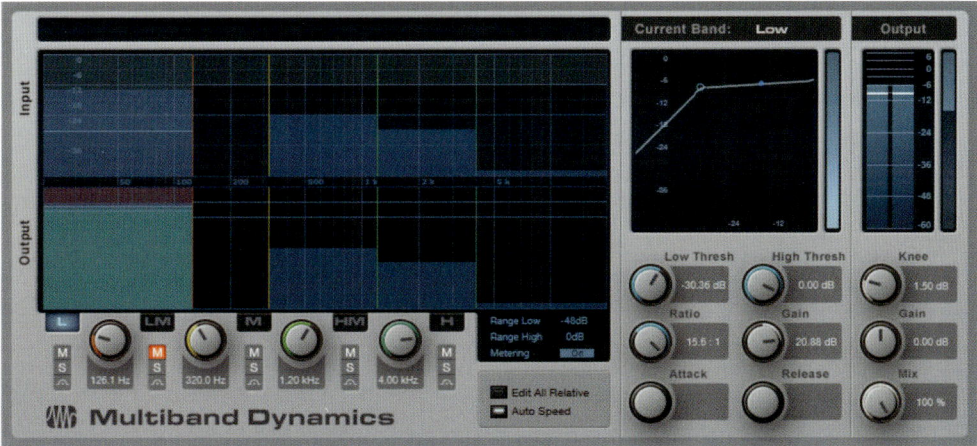

Figure 5.2 This screenshot shows the lowest band's parameter values, which create heavy compression.

As with any dynamic processing preset, the effect depends on the input level. For this preset, amplify the pre-EQ bass peaks as close to 0 dB as possible. For the low band, choose a ratio of 15:1, and a threshold of −30 dB. Mute the low mid band.

With the multiband dynamics processor bypassed, observe the peak value for the bass track. Next, enable multiband dynamics and adjust the low band's gain until the peak value matches the peak value with the multiband dynamics bypassed—you'll hear a big, fat, round bass sound that sort of tunnels through a mix.

Going to the other extreme, a significant upper midrange or treble boost can help a bass hold its own against other tracks, because the ear/brain combination will fill in the lower frequencies. Fig. 5.3 shows settings for extra articulation so that the bass "pops" and cuts through a track. Start with the default settings mentioned previously, but set the low band crossover frequency to 110 Hz or so.

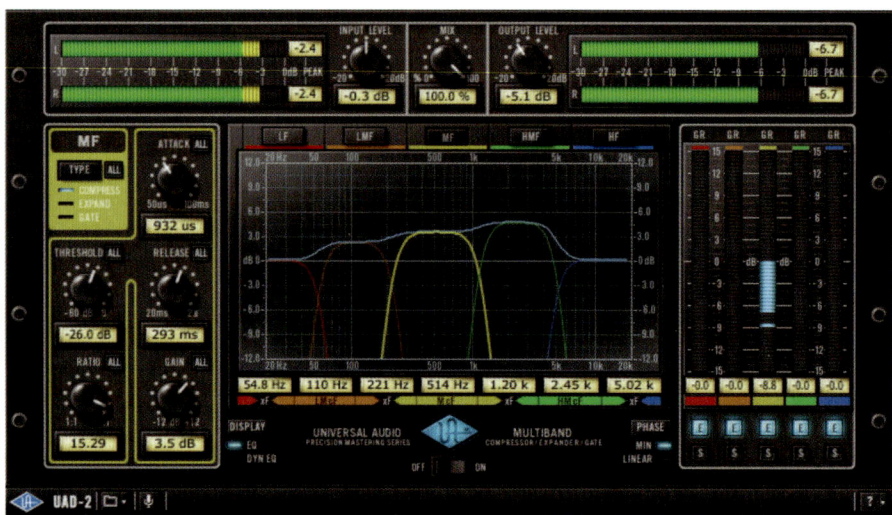

Figure 5.3 This use of multiband dynamics (with Universal Audio's Precision Multiband) for bass emphasizes articulation and pick attack. The screenshot shows the parameters for the all-important midrange band.

Only the mid band (320 to 1.2 kHz) is being compressed. A bit of uncompressed gain for the high mid band emphasizes pick noise and harmonics—about 5 dB or so seems about right. To compensate for the extra highs, add some gain (try 2 to 3 dB) to the low band around 110 Hz.

Most multiband dynamics processors have solo and mute buttons for individual stages. This makes it easy to assess the sonic contribution that each band makes.

Reduce Amp Sim Harshness with De-Essing

Feeding too much treble into an amp sim with a distorted sound can create a harsh, brittle timbre due to distorting the high frequencies. Although turning down your guitar's tone control can reduce highs, the tradeoff may be a more muffled sound. Fortunately, a de-esser provides an "intelligent" way to reduce the highs entering an amp sim by reducing high frequencies from your guitar when they're overly prominent, but otherwise leaving the signal unaffected. As a bonus, the compression contributed by de-essing adds smoothness.

Dedicated de-essers generally have a subset of a standard compressor's controls, with at least frequency and threshold parameters. Adjusting the parameters works similarly with all de-essers when applied to an amp sim.

The general process is as follows:

1. Start off with no filtering.

2. Set a de-esser threshold that's considerably lower than the high-frequency peaks, then define the high-frequency range that's being compressed. (Note that with some de-essers, the threshold control works in "reverse," with higher settings producing more compression.)

3. As you listen to the amp sim output while playing, at some point the sound will become sweeter as the highs start compressing.

4. If the de-essing effect is too obvious, raise the threshold and/or reduce the ratio (if present) to compensate.

A de-esser is useful beyond making sweeter distorted sounds. Vox AC-30 amp emulations have a naturally bright sound, so if you try to boost the treble too much, the sound becomes screechy. Use a de-esser to zero in on a narrow range of the brightest incoming frequencies (Fig. 5.4), reduce them, and then add EQ afterward to apply a wide treble boost. This gives a sweet but authoritative brightness that doesn't boost the harsh elements.

Figure 5.4 Inserting a de-esser before the ACE 30 amp in MOTU's Digital Performer gives a wonderfully bright but not overbearing Vox amp sound.

Dynamics Processing and Signal Chain Position

Dynamics processors typically insert in a mixer channel to process a recorded track. However, when dynamics are part of a chain of effects, the dynamics processor's position in that chain can have a major influence on the overall sound. Although many of these situations need handling on a case-by-case basis, some configurations are somewhat standard.

Dynamics Processing and EQ

There's no universal answer about whether dynamics processing should go before or after EQ. Both options have their uses.

Consider a synth bass line with a highly resonant filter sweep. On some notes, the level may go too high when a note's frequency coincides with the filter frequency. Suppose you want to boost the lower midrange a bit for a beefier sound. Place a limiter (or compressor) after the synth to trap those rogue transients, then apply EQ to the more dynamically consistent sound. If the EQ change is minor, it won't alter the signal's overall amplitude much.

Now suppose you don't have any problems with overly resonant filters, but you want a massive lower midrange boost. A large boost will increase the amplitude at some frequencies, so putting compression *after* EQ will help even out these level differences. However, there is a tradeoff. Because the EQ will be boosting in a certain frequency range, the compressor will scale those levels back down somewhat, depending on the threshold and ratio settings. So, this dilutes the effect of the EQ a bit—it wants to boost, but the compressor may act to turn down the boost.

Another use for EQ before compression is to make the compression more frequency–sensitive. To emphasize a guitar part's melody, boost EQ slightly for the range to be emphasized, and then compress. The boosted frequencies will cross over the compression threshold sooner than the other frequencies. Or, if a digital synth sounds "buzzy," cut the highs a bit prior to compression so the compressor will bring up other frequencies more readily than the highs. This type of technique isn't the same as multiband compression, but can give similar results.

Compression Before or After Distortion

Especially with guitar, compression before distortion gives a more sustained, even sound. Compression after distortion also evens out the sound, but it won't really give more sustain, and it will bring up any noise that's part of the compression process. However, if the distortion is simply some saturation on a recorded track, placing compression after the saturation can give the saturation more life. Noise probably won't be an issue if the saturation is mild.

Noise Gate Before or After Distortion

Noise gate before distortion is almost a given. Distortion reduces dynamic range, so the lower-level signals you want to eliminate will become fairly high in amplitude, and therefore, more difficult to remove without impacting the overall sound. Gating out low-level signals (like hum and noise) before they're distorted will prevent them from becoming amplified, and therefore, they won't compete with the overall sound. Unless the noise gate is being used as a special effect, insert it as close as possible to the signal chain's beginning.

Limiter Before or After Compressor

With vocals, I often place a limiter before the compressor to tame peaks. The compressor can then add light compression for a more natural sound, yet still deliver the needed amount of dynamics processing.

Limiter Before Amp Sim

Guitars are percussive instruments, with major peaks. Inserting a limiter before the amp sims feeds the sim a signal with more even dynamics, which produces a more consistent distortion sound.

Dynamics Control Before or After Envelope-Controlled Filter

An envelope-controlled filter depends on dynamics to alter the filter frequency; however sometimes the filter can be too sensitive, making it difficult to control the filter with your touch. Light compression or limiting before the filter can help tame the sensitivity, and paradoxically, make the filter sweep more responsive.

Conversely, dynamics control can also be helpful after an envelope-controlled filter to tame resonances, or produce a more consistent output level if the sound thins out at higher frequencies.

A Better Guitar Sustainer

This signal processing setup is optimized for single-string guitar solos with lots of sustain—but it incorporates a technique that creates a better effect than typical guitar stompbox sustainers.

A compressor is a guitar sustainer's main processor, and the settings are straightforward—a high compression ratio and low threshold (like 20:1 and −35 dB, respectively). A sharp knee lengthens the sustain time, while a short attack time clamps down the attack for a smoother sound. The release time isn't too critical, although this depends on your playing style; 300 to 500 ms usually works best.

This is an instance where you *don't* want to enable automatic or adaptive attack and release, because the goal *isn't* the most natural sound—it's an effect. However, enable lookahead if available, because it helps control the attack. Also note that because of the extreme compression, you'll need lots of makeup gain.

Unfortunately, a drawback with most sustainers is that after the release time ends, if there's a pause between notes, you'll hear a loud "pop" when the compression resumes upon playing a new note. A fast attack and lookahead helps, but it's almost impossible to avoid a nasty transient. Following the compressor with a distorted amp sim hides the pop somewhat, but still produces an ugly attack.

Inserting a transient shaper prior to the compressor (Fig. 5.5) will help tame the transients. This example uses Native Instruments' Transient Master and 160 Compressor. Pull the transient shaper's attack down to minimum, and reduce the sustain control (if present) as much as needed to help remove the pop. Even with an extremely low threshold and high compression ratio, this setup works well to give massive amounts of sustain, without an equally massive "pop" at the beginning of notes. You can use a distorted amp sim following this heavily sustained sound, and you'll still hear a cleaner attack.

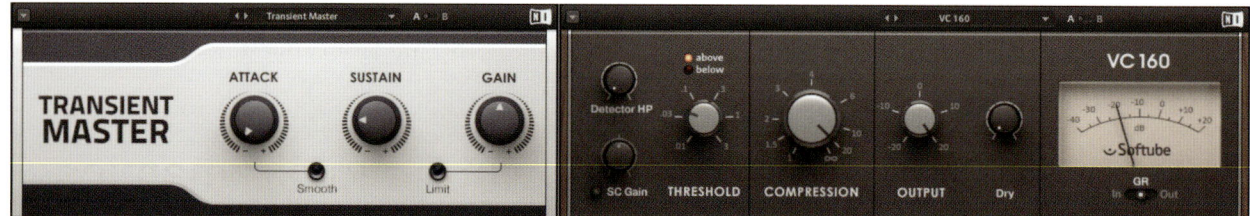

Figure 5.5 Adding a transient shaper prior to a compressor with heavy compression, and pulling down the attack and possibly the sustain as well, can minimize annoying pops at the beginning of notes.

Another option, albeit a less effective one, is to insert a noise gate before the compressor. Aside from the benefit of removing hum, noise, and other low-level signals from being compressed, if you add an attack time (55 ms seems about right), then when you hit a note after a pause, the note attack ramps up more slowly. The compressor can then "grab" the note without creating a pop. (Or if it does, the pop will be greatly reduced; note that depending on how fast you play, and the compressor's release time, you may need to edit the noise gate's release and hold times). The reason why this is less effective than a transient shaper is because it needs a pre-note pause for the gate to reset. A transient shaper will reduce all transients, regardless of when they're generated.

Noise Gate Attack Delay

An attack delay processor adds a slow, bowed-like attack to sounds with a fast attack (guitar, bass, organ, etc.). A noise gate with an attack parameter can provide this effect, but it requires silence just before the note where you want the slow attack time.

Setting the optimum threshold level and release time requires a tradeoff, because there must be a space before every note that needs an attack so the gate can reset back to being closed before it opens again. It helps to have a higher "off" threshold (i.e., where the gate closes) and a short release time, as this causes the preceding note to cut off sooner into silence. However, too short a release can result in a "chattering" effect, so use the shortest possible decay time consistent with a smooth sound and reliable triggering (a minimum hold time also helps). Then when you play a new note, the noise gate attack time will determine how long it takes for the signal to ramp up to full level. A typical setting is a few hundred milliseconds (Fig. 5.6).

Figure 5.6 Typical noise gate settings for an attack/delay effect.

If you don't want the new note to ramp up from 0 level, edit the noise gate depth control so the sound doesn't go fully silent after the signal passes below the threshold. In any event, the most dramatic effect occurs with the noise gate attenuation at maximum.

Interfacing Electric Instruments with Studio Dynamics Processors

"Stomp box" dynamics processors are more limited than rack-mount studio hardware—but the latter have level issues with guitar, bass, electric piano, and other electric instruments because there can be impedance and level mismatches. Interfacing involves one of three approaches.

Use an instrument input, if available. If the processor has an "instrument" input (unlikely, but possible), that's all you need. Plug the instrument directly into the processor, then run the processor's output into the mixer, patch bay, amp modeler, or even a guitar amp (assuming you can adjust the output level to avoid overloading the guitar amp—unless that's what you want).

Tech Talk: What's the Optimum Instrument Impedance?

An instrument input impedance above 100 kilohms, and preferably above 220 kilohms, will avoid dulling high frequencies and reducing the level with passive pickups. But too high an impedance (in the 5 to 10 megohm range) reaches a point of diminishing returns, because now the input may be too sensitive and prone to noise pickup. A 1 megohm impedance is a good compromise setting, but any impedance above 500K will likely not create any audible degradation to the guitar signal.

Active pickups do not require an instrument impedance to preserve tone, but they may benefit from one anyway, because the output may not reach line levels and may require the additional amplification an instrument input can provide.

Use a preamp or suitable direct box. Inserting a preamp or direct box (with an appropriately high input impedance) after the instrument, but before the dynamics processor, will preserve the guitar signal's fidelity.

With a hardware mixer, insert the dynamics processor into your mixer's channel inserts. This will also match levels properly, although you'll still need to decide how to interface the guitar with the mixer. The choices are the same as above: If the mixer has an instrument input, great. If not, use a device like a preamp or direct box between the guitar and mixer.

Transparent Compression

Inserting two compressors in series, with both set for low compression ratios and high thresholds, can sound less obvious than using a single compressor to produce the same apparent amount of compression. The first stage essentially "pre-conditions" the signal so that the second compressor doesn't have to work so hard (Fig. 5.7).

Figure 5.7 These two PSP Audioware compressors are in series, with gentle compression settings to give transparent compression effects.

With a hardware stereo compressor capable of dual mono operation, you can patch a mono signal through the two individual compression channels in series. With plug-ins, for either mono or stereo signals, insert two compressors in series in a track.

The drawback is that, unlike standard compression, two sets of controls now require adjustment instead of just one. However, most of the time you'll set them to similar settings anyway, or leave the first compressor at a fixed amount, and vary only the second compressor's controls. Experiment with the knee settings, as softer, more rounded knees can give a more subtle effect.

Some virtual studio software can create effects *chains* that serve as "containers" for multiple effects. You can then assign their parameters to macro knobs that control several parameters at once. For example, a ratio control could control the ratio in both compressors simultaneously.

A One-Knob Compressor

Speaking of effects chains and macro controls, here's an example of how to make a one-knob compressor that alters multiple parameters at once. Although this isn't as versatile as tweaking individual parameters, it allows setting up a "close enough" sound within seconds—maybe you're tracking and want to compress the vocals in the monitor mix, or hear what the bass will sound like when you add some compression on mixdown. Rather than divert your attention with tweaking, sometimes it's a lot easier to insert a one-knob compressor temporarily for a quick adjustment, and save the hardcore tweaking for when it's time to mix.

Waves makes a one-knob compressor plug-in, but Studio One or Cakewalk by BandLab users can take advantage of effects chains to create a one-knob compressor that sweeps from no compression, to some compression, to compression that's more like a guitar sustainer stompbox (Fig. 5.8).

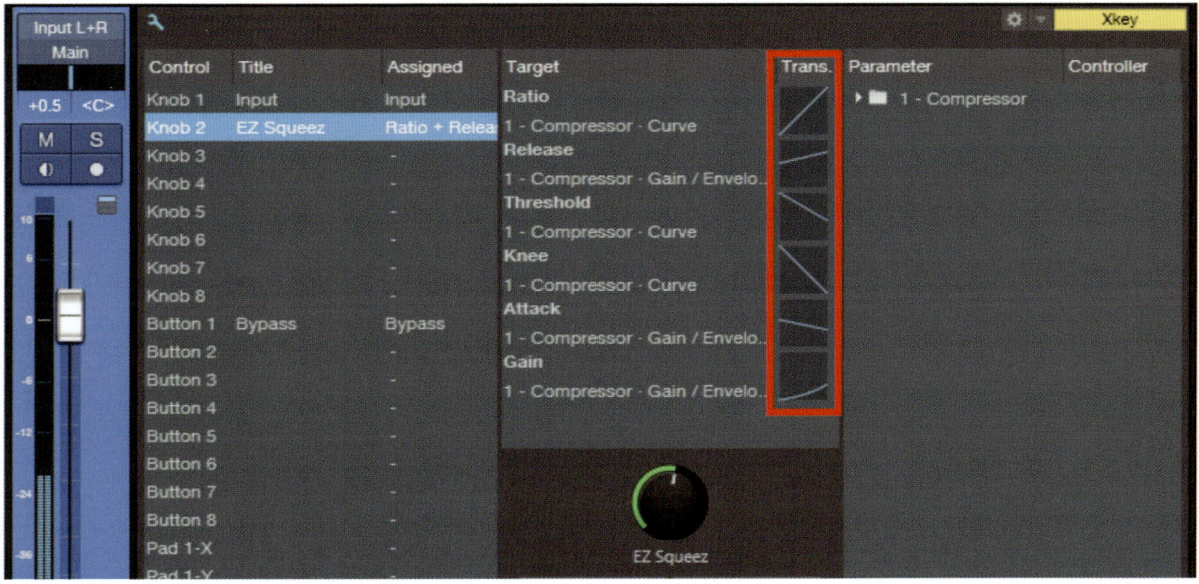

Figure 5.8 A single knob controls ratio, release, threshold, knee, attack, and gain. The thumbnails next to the parameters (outlined in red) show how the parameter values change as you turn up the knob.

As the ratio increases, release increases somewhat, threshold goes lower, the knee gets harder, attack decreases a bit, and the gain goes up semi-exponentially to compensate for the lower threshold and higher ratio.

Fig. 5.9 shows how the compressor settings change for three different macro control positions (for clarity, parameters not relevant to this technique aren't shown).

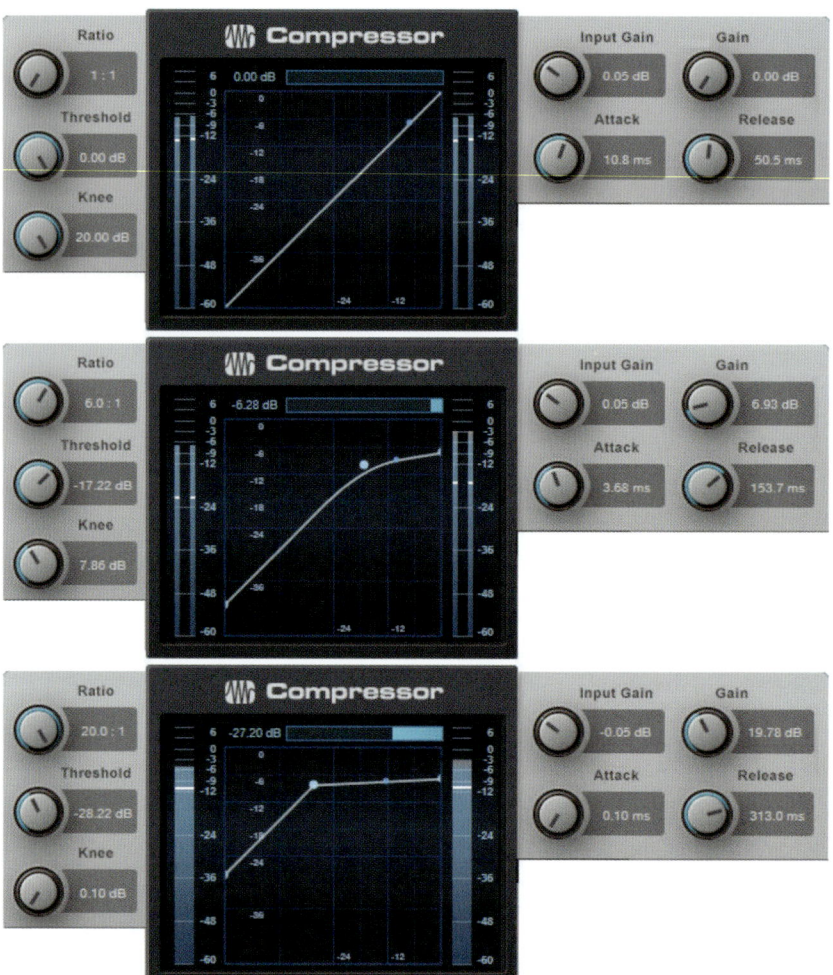

Figure 5.9 The top settings reflect the macro knob turned fully counter-clockwise (minimal compression). The middle image shows the settings with the knob turned up about 60%. The lower image shows settings with the knob all the way up.

Because compressors are so dependent on the input signal level, I added an input level control so the input could be trimmed for the compressor's "sweet spot." There's also a bypass button to compare the compressed and uncompressed sounds.

Knob settings between 30% and 65% will work for a variety of signal sources. Past 65%, the compressor enters a more extreme territory that pumps mixed drums, and acts more like a sustainer for guitar. But it's easy enough to find what works best with a one-knob compressor: just turn the knob until the compression sounds right.

Sidechain Applications

Because sidechaining takes over the dynamics control for compressors, limiters, and noise gates, it allows for a wide variety of creative applications.

Locking Kick Drum and Bass Together

For an ultra-tight rhythm section, you can lock the bass to the kick so that the bass plays only when the kick drum hits (Fig. 5.10).

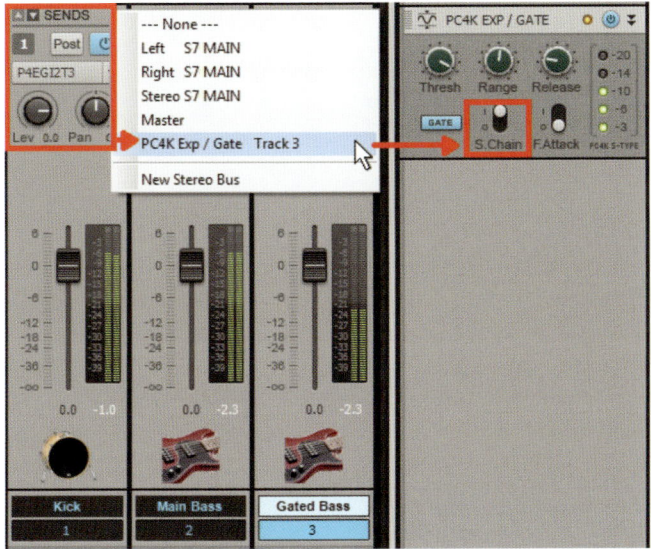

Figure 5.10 Track setup for locking bass to drums. The kick send is pre-fader (i.e., its level is independent of the channel fader), and goes to the sidechain-enabled Expander/Gate that's inserted in the Gated Bass track.

Set the gate's threshold so that it opens when the kick exceeds the threshold. The gate's range control could mute bass completely when the kick doesn't hit, or let through some of the bass part. Release can add a tasty bass decay that lasts longer than the kick, thereby differentiating the two instruments a bit more.

Pumped Drums

This turns dynamics control on its head by *encouraging* the sound to "pump," rather than sound natural. However, the sound is very different compared to using lots of compression with a really high ratio.

Sidechaining is a key component in this popular dance music effect that was highlighted in Eric Prydz's seminal EDM video from 2004, "Call on Me." The setup is a bit complicated (Fig. 5.11), but it's worth the effort. Note that this effect works best if there are some sustaining sounds that it can pump—like cymbals for drum parts, or pads if you want to pump a non-drum track.

78 How to Apply Dynamics Processing

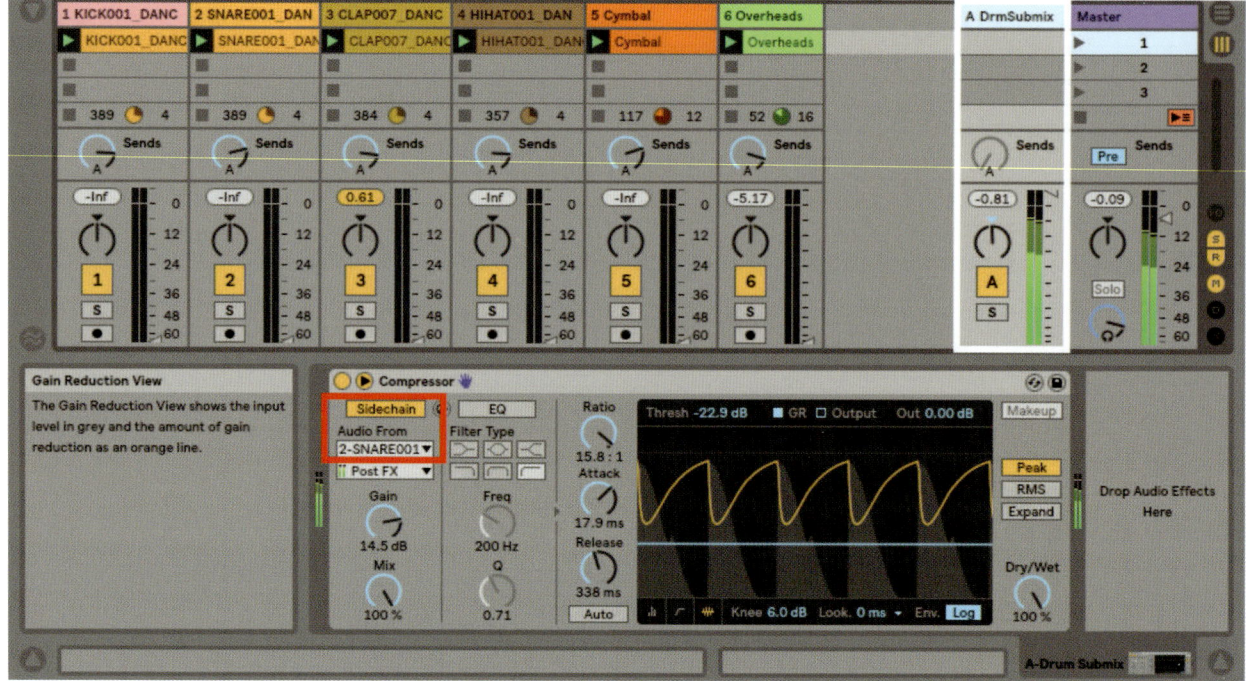

Figure 5.11 In Ableton Live, the snare track feeds the drum submix compressor's sidechain input (outlined in red), so it alone controls the compressor's dynamics. The orange line shows the amount of gain reduction being applied to the compressor from the snare.

To set up a sidechain effect, do the following:

1. Send the drum tracks to a drum submix bus (in Figure 5.11, the bus is labeled A DrmSubmix and is outlined in white).

2. Assign the drum submix output to your main stereo out bus.

3. Insert a compressor with sidechaining in the drum submix bus.

4. Set the compressor for heavy compression—e.g., threshold below −20 and a ratio higher than 10:1.

5. Assign the sidechain input to the snare (or kick, or whatever...take your pick). With some programs, you may need to assign the sidechain source to a bus or output, and assign the sidechain target to that bus or output.

6. Start with the compression attack time set to 0 ms; the drum sound will essentially disappear when the snare hits because the gain is being reduced so much. Gradually increase the attack time to let through more of the initial snare hit, and add some release time (250 to 500 ms) to increase the apparent amount of pumping.

Frequency-Selective Compression

Some instruments lack "sparkle" when compressed because the stronger lower frequencies trigger compression that affects the high frequencies as well. This is a common problem with guitar, but using sidechain techniques can compress only the guitar's lower frequencies, while leaving the higher frequencies uncompressed. (Multiband compression works for this too, but sometimes, sidechaining offers more flexibility in controlling frequencies than a multiband compressor.) Frequency-selective compression can also be effective with drums, dance mixes, and more.

One frequency-selective compression method uses a compressor that accommodates inserting a filter in the internal sidechain (Fig. 5.12)

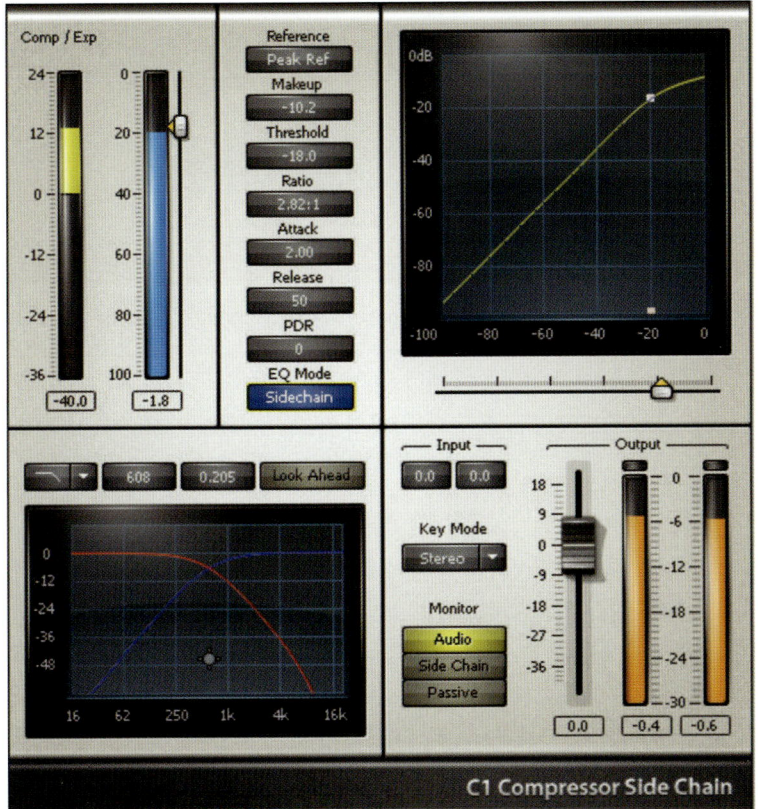

Figure 5.12 Waves C1 Compressor Side Chain includes an internal filter for the sidechain. This application is applying compression only to the lower frequencies.

If a compressor lacks internal sidechain filtering, note that you usually can't sidechain a track to itself, because this could cause a feedback loop. So, another option is copying a track for use solely as a sidechain control signal (Fig. 5.13).

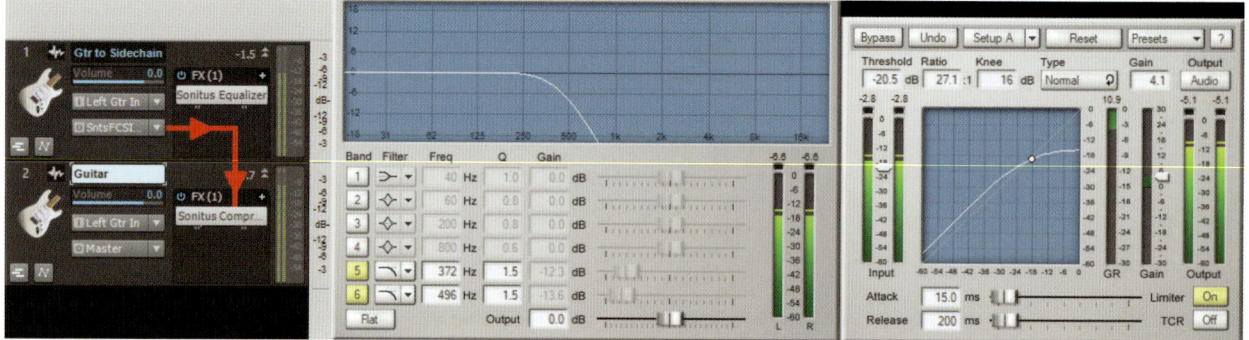

Figure 5.13 In Cakewalk by BandLab, the low-pass equalizer filters out the highs going to the compressor's sidechain input, which restricts compression to only the lower frequencies.

To configure frequency-selective compression, do the following:

1. Copy the track with the sound to be processed so two tracks are playing the same part (in the screenshot, the upper, copied track provides the sidechain signal).

2. Insert a compressor in the main track.

3. Insert an equalizer in the copied track, then assign its track output to the sidechain input for the compressor in the main guitar track.

4. Use the equalizer's low-pass filter to trim the high frequencies. The example shown here stacks two low-pass filters for a steeper response.

5. Adjust the compressor for the desired amount of compression. This will affect only the low frequencies.

Being able to monitor the sidechain signal is important when doing frequency-selective compression, so you can tune the filter properly. With hardware units, there's usually a monitor button. With a sidechain-friendly software compressor, use the Key Input, Listen, Audition, or similar function to hear the results of changing the EQ's frequency.

Frequency-Selective Drum Pumping

Frequency-selective compression can provide a pumping effect even more drastic than the one mentioned previously, if you're working with a full, mixed drum part. As with the above tip, you can't sidechain a track by itself, so here's another way to accomplish what we want (Fig. 5.14). This time we'll key off the kick instead of the snare.

Dynamics Processor Applications

Figure 5.14 In Cubase, the equalizer in the copied drum track (outlined in orange) tunes out everything except the kick drum. The main drum track to its right goes through a compressor with an enabled sidechain input. Creating a pre-fader send in the copied drum track, and assigning it to the compressor sidechain, causes the kick to control the compressor.

To configure frequency-selective compression for drums:

1. Copy the track with the drum part so you have two tracks playing the same part.
2. Insert a compressor in the main drum track.
3. Insert an equalizer in the second drum track.
4. Temporarily solo the second drum track and set its output to the master bus so you can hear it.
5. Tweak the second drum track's EQ to tune out everything but the kick drum. A resonant low-pass filter, or a combination of a low-pass filter with a parametric stage to boost the kick, should do the job. Once that's set, assign the track output (or a pre-fader send from the track) to the compressor's sidechain input, and turn off the copied track's solo button.
6. Adjust the compressor for the desired sound. Start with attack at minimum, and release for the desired amount of pumping—try between 100 and 300 ms, depending on the song and the material. To restore some of the attack at the start of the pumping, increase the attack time. Even a little bit, like 5 ms, restores most of the attack's effect.

The effect's depth, like any compression effect, depends on the threshold and ratio settings. For a heavy-duty effect, set threshold between −20 and −30 dB and the ratio around 10:1. You'll want to tweak the settings depending on the program material, but these will provide a good starting point. Finally, because this effect does compress, some makeup gain will be needed.

Ducking a Music Bed with Narration

Let's use the example of narration lowering the level of a music bed whenever the narrator speaks. This is a good application for a noise gate (if it has a ducking mode—few do), a dedicated ducking effect, or a compressor, which is what we'll use. Note that the same principle works if, for example, you want to lower a rhythm guitar's volume when the vocals come in.

1. Insert a compressor in the music bed track.
2. Add a send to the vocal track, and assign the send to the compressor sidechain input.
3. Edit the compressor parameters so that the vocal track reduces the music bed by the desired amount.

Getting the right effect is tricky. For a smooth ducking action, set the attack time around 100 ms so the ducking doesn't hit instantly. Also try a fairly long release, like 200 ms or more; however, too long a release will sound like an obvious effect, not the music bed fading back in smoothly. A soft knee response can also give a smoother ducking effect.

The threshold will be relatively low because you want a soft voice to trigger the compression. Too high a ratio will give an unnatural sound. Typically, you'll reduce the music by only a few dB, because that will be sufficient to keep the music bed from overpowering the narration (Fig. 5.15).

Figure 5.15 Pro Tools is set up for ducking a music bed with narration. The narration uses a send (in this case, Bus 7) to trigger the sidechain of the compressor inserted in the music bed track.

Gentler Sidechain Gating

I've always been fascinated with using one instrument to control another instrument—like using a vocoder on guitar or pads, but with drums as the modulator instead of voice. This kind of processing is a natural for dance music, and using a noise gate's sidechain to gate one instrument with another (e.g., bass gated by kick drum, as described previously) is a common technique.

However, the sound of gating has always seemed somewhat abrupt, regardless of how I tweaked a gate's attack, decay, threshold, and range parameters. I wanted something a little more natural, with more flexibility. The solution is unconventional… but try it.

As illustrated in Figure 5.16, to set this up you will copy the track you want to modulate (in this case, track 3, RhyGtr1; the copy is track 4, RhyGtr1 2). Then, flip the copy's audio 180 degrees out of phase (i.e., invert the polarity). This is the purpose of the Mixtool processor, and it causes the audio from the original track and its copy to cancel.

Figure 5.16 The setup for a gentler sidechaining effect.

Next, insert a compressor in the copied track, and feed its sidechain with a send from the track doing the modulating. In this case, it's the drum track at the top of Figure 5.16.

When compression happens, it reduces the gain of the out-of-phase audio, thus reducing the amount of cancellation. However, the gain changes don't have the same character as gating—the sound is smoother and "gentler."

You can take this technique further with automation. The screenshot shows automation that's adjusting the compressor's threshold; the lower the threshold, the less cancellation. Raising the threshold determines when the "gating" effect occurs. Also, it's worth experimenting with the compressor's attack and release parameters.

Using a compressor for pseudo-gating allows for flexibility that isn't possible when adjusting a standard noise gate. For a super-tight rhythmic sync between two instruments, this is an unusual—but useful—alternative to sidechain-based gating.

The Compressor/Limiting "Delta" Test

A variation of the "Gentler Sidechain Gating" technique can also give insights into how a compressor affects a track.

1. Duplicate the track that contains the compressor, with identical compressor and level settings.
2. Flip the polarity (phase) on the copied track. The sound should cancel because the two tracks are out of phase.
3. With the compressor in the copied track, change the ratio to 1:1 (1.0). This prevents it from compressing the signal.
4. Because the tracks are out of phase, now you will hear only the effect that the compressor has on the sound (Fig. 5.17).

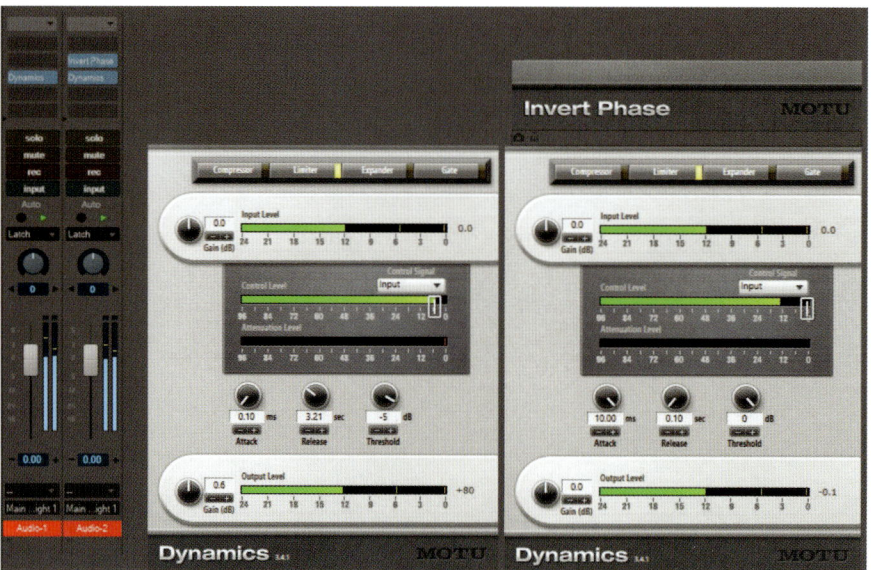

Figure 5.17 This test setup in MOTU Digital Performer allows evaluating how the compressor is affecting the sound. The compressor on the right is in the copied track, and has default settings. The compressor on the left has some parameter changes, so we can hear the results of those changes.

Listen carefully to the resulting sound. You'll hear if the compression has an elegant entrance and exit as it starts compressing the signal, as well as the audible results of attack and release control settings (which may be difficult to hear otherwise). This also makes the knee's influence on the sound obvious, as well as the difference between manual and attack/release auto adjustments.

Note that this works best with compressors that have an auto-gain option. Otherwise, you may need to adjust the compressed track's output to hear more accurately how the compression affects the sound.

Drum Enhancement

Here's yet another use for sidechain-triggered gating. The following technique works well for giving snare a more "80s" drum sound.

1. Create a track with white or pink noise for the length of the drum part.
2. Insert an EQ in the track to shape the noise's tone as desired.
3. Follow the EQ with a gate.
4. Add a send from the snare drum track and assign it to the noise gate's sidechain input.
5. The noise will now trigger when the snare drum hits. Adjust the gate's attack and decay so that the noise's dynamics follow the snare drum.

You can also enhance a kick drum with a similar technique, but instead of creating a track with white noise, create a track with a steady sine wave (50 to 70 Hz or so). Insert a gate in this track, and trigger its sidechain input with the kick drum. Set a fairly high threshold, and use the gate's decay control to set the sine wave's decay time.

You can create even more interesting sounds when you trigger effects on one drum from a different drum. Here's one of my favorites, if you have snare and kick on separate tracks.

1. Create a bus with reverb that has a long decay time (like 10 seconds).
2. Create a send from the snare track that goes to the reverb.
3. Insert a gate after the reverb. Set its attack and hold times to 20 ms and its release to around 250 ms.
4. Create a send from the kick drum track and assign it to the gate's sidechain input.

Now the kick drum will gate the snare's reverb, producing twisted rhythmic effects.

Key Takeaways

- There are reasons why you may not want to compress the master bus when mixing.

- People generally think of multiband dynamics as applicable mostly to program material, but it can also enhance individual instruments like bass.

- De-essing has benefits for more than just vocals, such as helping create sweeter amp sim sounds.

- In a chain of effects, the position where you insert the dynamics processing (beginning, middle, or end of the chain) makes a difference in the overall sound.

- Transient shapers can tame a guitar's strong transients, which often improves the sound with compressors and amp sims.

- Noise gates can serve as attack delay processors, where a signal fades in over time.

- Electric instruments such as guitar can work with studio-oriented hardware processors, but they require proper impedance and level matching.

- Having two compressors in series set for light compression can give a more transparent sound than a single compressor set to provide a similar amount of compression.

- By using effects chains and macro controls, it's possible to create a versatile, single-knob compressor.

- Sidechaining can make bass and kick drum lock together tightly.

- Sidechaining is the basis of the popular "pumping" effect for drums that you'll hear in some EDM productions.

- Frequency-selective compression takes advantage of sidechaining, and with some compressors, can be implemented internally (no external sidechain control required). In other situations, it may be necessary to copy an audio track and use it to provide the sidechain audio.

- Reducing the level of a music bed during narration is another application for sidechaining.

- There's a simple diagnostic technique to hear how compression affects a sound.

- Sidechaining can gate another sound along with drums to reinforce the drum sound (like gating a sine wave with a kick drum, or white noise with snare).

Appendix

The "Loudness Wars" and Measuring Dynamics

The music industry's "loudness wars," where everyone wanted THE LOUDEST POSSIBLE RECORDING, has resulted in a lot of collateral damage—like a dramatically reduced dynamic range, which takes out an emotionally important musical component. The loudness wars happened because people generally perceive music that's louder as being better: if two songs in a playlist are played back to back, and the second one is louder, it seems just a little better (Fig. A.1).

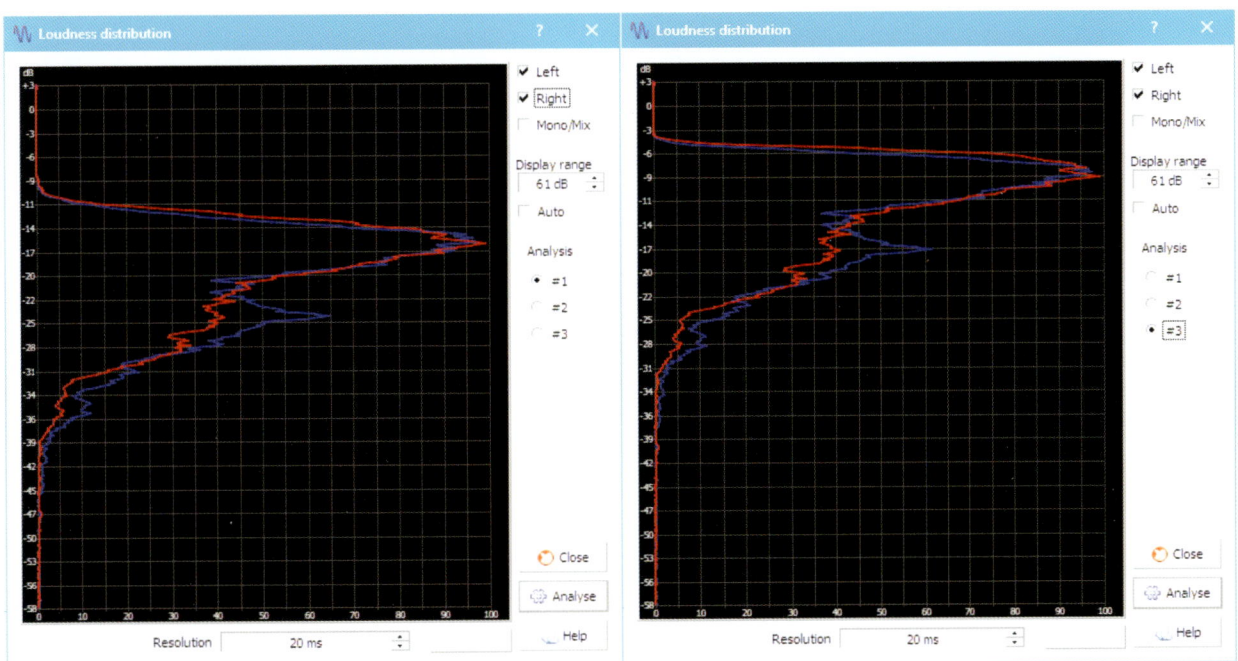

Figure A.1 The histogram shows loudness distribution at different levels. The image on the left shows a file before the effect of the loudness wars; its loudest peaks occur at −17 dB. The image on the right has been maximized for more level, and the loudest peaks occur at −9 dB. That's quite a bit louder.

There's also a physical reason people may prefer the sound of loud music: the ear has a flatter response at higher levels. At lower levels, the high and low frequencies aren't as prominent.

However, losing dynamics for the sake of volume is not a good tradeoff. To level the playing field, the European Broadcast Union standardized on a method to measure perceived loudness and dynamic range. By doing so, broadcasters could easily adjust the levels of different pieces of music—whether they had a wide or narrow dynamic range—to sound *subjectively* as if they had the same loudness. This allows you to create music with a wide dynamic range, yet not have it sound "weak" compared to other music.

Measuring Dynamics

There are two traditional ways to measure audio levels: peak and RMS (Root Mean Square). Peak measures the highest level that the audio produces, while RMS measures the average level. RMS correlates more closely to our hearing.

For example, a snare drum hit has a high peak value with a rapid decay, while a sustained power chord has a high average value. The power chord will sound subjectively louder even if its peak isn't as high. If you adjust both to the same RMS level, their levels will sound more evenly matched.

We now have a new way to measure levels: the loudness unit. Basically, this involves loudness meters that go far beyond conventional VU or peak meters. The most common measurement based on loudness units is called LUFS, which stands for Loudness Unit Full Scale. Steinberg Cubase, PreSonus Studio One, Apple Logic, MAGIX Samplitude, iZotope Insight, and other programs now include this type of metering.

In a nutshell, this measures a piece of music's *perceived* loudness. In theory, two pieces of music that register identical LUFS readings should sound like they're at the same level, and in practice, they do indeed sound like they're at the same subjective level, regardless of the dynamics (which are preserved—one of the main benefits of using LUFS). One immediate, practical benefit that doesn't relate to broadcasting is for mastering when you want consistent levels among tracks—you just need to check their LUFS readings.

LUFS readings are represented by a negative number, like –5 LUFS, –10 LUFS, –13 LUFS, etc. The higher the value, the higher the average level. But here's the beauty of the system: a given broadcaster can decide on a standard LUFS level (YouTube uses –13 LUFS; Spotify uses –14 LUFS, iTunes Radio uses around –16 LUFS) so that people don't have to turn the volume up and down constantly. All that's needed is for the broadcaster or streaming service to adjust the audio's level to the same LUFS reading. Sure, you can still squash the living daylights out of your audio and generate something that's –5 LUFS, but when YouTube gets ahold of it, it will be dialed back to –13 LUFS anyway, so it's the same apparent level as everything else. Similarly, if you have a jazz track with a wide dynamic range that registers –18 LUFS, its level will be raised to –13 LUFS on YouTube. So, a hardcore Belgian techno track from 1990 will have the same perceived level as a live jazz recording. This means there's no longer any reason to participate in the loudness wars.

For broadcast, the recommended standard for audio is –23 LUFS—but that's different from mastering music for playback. We often make subjective calls about the desired amount of dynamic range, and can master to whatever LUFS we want. With CDs, you can go as high as your bad taste will allow, but I think higher than –9 LUFS loses most of the dynamic range.

For club tracks you might want to master to a higher average level, like −6 LUFS, because there's no standard level for clubs like there is for broadcasters or streaming services. But again, when your track gets broadcast, it will have the same perceived level as other music.

Measuring with the LUFS algorithm involves more than just sticking a meter on something, because it takes into account fades and quiet passages. Fortunately, all the deep computational work happens in the background.

More Metering

Two other readings can help gauge dynamic range. These provide data that may cause you to go back and make some changes in the track levels or dynamics (Fig. A.2).

Figure A.2 Three files from my "Joie de Vivre" project (youtube.com/thecraiganderton) have been mastered, but as the waveforms show, don't have consistent levels. The Waves L3 Multimaximizer allows tweaking the perceived level for consistency. After these tweaks, all three tracks now measure −11.4 LUFS. The following text explains the purpose of the other readings.

LRA is a reading of dynamic range. The typical range is from 5 (very little dynamic range, like a commercial or aggressive club mix) to 15 (a live acoustic recording). This is more like a reality check. Most of my music has a dynamic range rating of 8 or 9, which leans toward a somewhat limited dynamic range so the music "pops" a little more. However, I noticed one song was a 6, so I looked at it further, even though subjectively, it seemed to be the same level as the other tracks. It was a dance mix that truly didn't have a lot of dynamic range in the parts themselves, so I didn't make any changes… but it's helpful to get that kind of feedback.

TP stands for "true peak," and it takes intersample distortion into account (i.e., the distortion that can occur when reconstructing the signal through a D/A converter's smoothing filter, even though a peak meter that measures sample levels doesn't show distortion). This is important because you don't want your dynamics to have peaks that are sufficiently loud to create distortion. TP readings should be –0.1 dB or lower.

Yes, Dynamics are Back

Purists can get upset that we're turning our subjective evaluations of levels over to an algorithm. But frankly, it's an effective algorithm. It used to take me hours to balance levels on an album. Now it takes about 30 minutes (including custom tweaking), with excellent results, because there's numeric feedback on the levels that makes for easy level matching.

Granted, the album format isn't as popular as it once was, but song collections still are, and LUFS metering can help guarantee consistent levels. But perhaps more importantly, in today's singles-oriented world, LUFS means an end to the loudness wars—you can't crank the maximizer up to 11 and have your song sound louder on YouTube, because YouTube will just turn it back down again. And if you appreciate music with dynamic range, YouTube will make sure it sounds subjectively as loud as everything else… just with more dynamic range. This is indeed progress.

About the Author

Musician/author Craig Anderton is an internationally recognized authority on music and technology. His onstage career spans from the 60s with the group Mandrake, through the early 2000s with electronic groups Air Liquide and Rei$$dorf Force, to the "power duo" EV2 with Public Enemy's Brian Hardgroove, and EDM-oriented solo performances.

He has played on, produced, or mastered over 20 major label recordings, did pop music session work in New York in the 1970s on guitar and keyboards, played Carnegie Hall, and more recently, has mastered well over a hundred tracks for various artists.

In the mid-80s, Craig co-founded *Electronic Musician* magazine. As an author, he's written over 35 books on musical electronics and over a thousand articles for magazines like *Keyboard, Sound on Sound, Rolling Stone, Pro Sound News, Guitar Player, Mix,* and several European publications.

Craig has lectured on technology and the arts (in 10 countries, 38 U.S. states, and three languages), and done sound design work for companies like Alesis, Gibson, Peavey, PreSonus, Roland, and Steinberg.

Please check out some of his music at youtube.com/thecraiganderton, visit his web site at craiganderton.com, and follow him on twitter @craig_anderton.